CYCLING ALONG THE CANALS OF NEW YORK

500 MILES OF BIKE RIDING
ALONG THE ERIE, CHAM-
PLAIN, CAYUGA-SENECA, AND
OSWEGO CANALS

CYCLING ALONG THE CANALS OF NEW YORK

500 MILES OF BIKE RIDING ALONG THE ERIE, CHAMPLAIN, CAYUGA-SENECA, AND OSWEGO CANALS

Louis Rossi

VITESSE PRESS • COLLEGE PARK, MARYLAND

Published by Vitesse Press
4431 Lehigh Road, #288
College Park, MD 20740

Library of Congress Cataloging-in-Publication Data

Rossi, Louis.
  Cycling along the canals of New York : 500 miles of bike riding
along the Erie, Champlain, Cayuga-Seneca, and Oswego canals /
Louis Rossi
    p. cm.
  ISBN 0-941950-35-2 (alk. paper)
    1. New York (State)—Guidebooks. 2. Canals—New York
(State—Guidebooks. 3. Trails—New York (State) —Guidebooks.
4. Cycling—New York (State)—Guidebooks. I. Title

  F117.3.R67 1998
  917.4704'43 —dc21   98-30952
                                                              CIP

Cover design by James Brisson

Cover photograph of Lockport, New York — Niagara County , Department of
Planning, Development & Tourism

Manufactured in the United States of America

10 9 8 7 6 5 4 3 2 1

Distributed in the United States by Alan C. Hood, Inc. (717-267-0867)

For sales inquiries and special prices for bulk quantities, contact Vitesse Press at
301-772-5915 or write to the address above.

Notice

This book is designed to help you enjoy cycling trips on the roads and trails along New York's canals. It is not intended as a substitute for proper planning nor as a current description of riding surfaces and auto traffic. As with any cycling trip, you should wear a helmet and ride with caution. A good cyclist knows the rules of the road and obeys them. On the road or on the path, be courteous to all users. Set a good example — courtesy is contagious.

CONTENTS

DEDICATION

To state employees. First, to the many canal employees of the New York State Department of Transportation, who, during the 1970s struggled to keep New York's canals open and functioning, when it was not in fashion and against all odds. You preserved the canals until they could be rediscovered and rescued. Next, to the many employees of the Office of State Park and Recreation, Canal Corporation, and NYSDOT who, today, keep our historic sites, canals, and excellent roads open to enjoy. This is "our tax dollars at work." Thank you.

INTRODUCTION

A little bit of New York history
...starting with the last ice-age...

This tour bicycles through New York's history. As you follow the route of New York's canals, you will learn more about New York in the last four centuries than could possibly be described here. You will also learn how geography, which facilitated "water level" or river-based transportation, fostered the creation of the powerful Iroquois Confederacy. You'll also see how it enabled the Dutch, British and American commerce of the region to expand, turning the colony of New York, as George Washington suggested, into "the Empire State."

So if geography shaped the history of the region, what shaped New York's geography? Let's go back to the last ice age for that answer. About 10,000 years ago, and for thousands of years before that, what is now New York State was totally covered by ice ranging from a mile to two miles in thickness. Imagine the polar ice cap extending to present day New York City. As they expanded and retreated, the glaciers determined every natural feature that we see in New York State. Beneath the ice, the land was being "scoured" by ice and debris, resulting in today's river valleys and lakes that form the core of our bike tour.

Much of what man made in New York exploited what nature left. The Iroquois used the glacially-shaped river valleys and lakes for transportation and commerce and located their major villages on hilltops at the junctions of natural waterways. The many canals of New York State, particularly the Erie and Champlain, were only possible because the last ice age scoured navigable passes through the Appalachian chain of mountains. These nearly sea-level passes are unique in Eastern America. The Hudson River at Albany is an ocean port and is tidal; the Indians called it "the river that flows two ways." New York City skyscrapers were an engineering possibility because the glaciers exposed hard metamorphic rock, perfect for supporting foundations. The great deep-water harbor of New York, perhaps the greatest natural harbor in the world, is also a result of glaciation.

Because of this glaciation, transportation was relatively easy in this part of the colonies. There were no mountains to climb; small boats and canoes could go almost anywhere. The Indians let the impenetrable forests define the boundaries of their territories, more-or-less content to use the waterways to define their nations. However, when these forests became the unmarked border between French Canada and English America, border disputes began. New York's waterways were the route of warfare for over 100 years. Consequently, as you bike along the canals of New York, you will be traversing historic sites from the French and Indian War, the Revolutionary War, and the War of 1812.

Beginning in the late 1600s, there were a series of wars known collectively as "the French and Indian Wars." They took place along the vague boundaries between the French settlements along the Saint Lawrence River in Canada and the British colonies along the Atlantic. To a great extent, this involved the Upper Hudson River, Mohawk River, and Lake Champlain regions. The cost of winning these wars, imposed upon the colonies by Great Britain, was a principal cause of the American Revolution. Much of that war, particularly events leading up to the decisive Battle of Saratoga, took place across the Hudson, Mohawk, and Champlain Valleys too. You will find, as you pedal along New York's canals, that several key battles of the War of 1812 were fought along these crucial waterways. You'll also learn that American troops, hoping to add to the Union, travelled north by water to invade Canada. (Even after the War of 1812, the precise location of the border was unclear and the Americans built "Fort Blunder" just north of Rouses Point, inside Canada.)

Yet, despite this bloody history, when peace arrived in 1815, and the borders were finally set, it would be only two years until groundbreaking for the Erie Canal and ten years until its completion and opening in 1825. Thus began an era of water-borne commerce, which helped shape not only the Empire State, but also the nation — an era that continues today.

Today, the Erie Canal and the other canals that comprise the New York State Canal System remain open and in use. They are an outstanding recreational resource. As you get ready to go, you might recall what James Fennimore Cooper says when writing about the Champlain Canal in The Last of the Mohicans:

The tourist......who, in the train of his four-in-hand, now rolls through the scenes we have attempted to describe, in quest of information, health, or pleasure, or floats steady toward his object on those artificial waters which have sprung up under the administration of a statesman [De Witt Clinton] *who has dared to stake his political character on the hazardous issue, is not to suppose that his ancestors traversed those hills, or struggled with the same currents with equal facility. The transportation of a single heavy gun was often considered equal to a victory gained....*

Pedaling the routes along New York's canals combines safe and scenic rides, both on-road and along the canal towpaths, with incredible opportunity for insight into early American history. Let's get started.

HOW TO USE
THIS GUIDEBOOK

Early in the historical novel, <u>The Last of the Mohicans</u>, Major Heyward, after being deliberately led astray along the upper Hudson River (Near today's Lake Champlain Feeder Canal Trail—See Chapter 5) by the evil Huron warrior Magua, and found by Hawkeye, Uncas and Chingachgook, asks:

"…what is our distance from the main army at Edward?"
Hawkeye replies:
"It seems that may depend on who is your guide."

Major Heyward was unaccustomed to the wilderness and needed three guides. I am going to offer you three guides as well — not to help you through the wilderness, but to aid you in fully exploring the complex and exciting history of New York. Your guides will be:

• Bike Routes "5" and "9," recently opened by the New York State Department of Transportation. Bike Route "5" extends East-West across the State from Albany to Buffalo, and was laid out to closely follow the Erie Canal. Bike Route "9" extends North-South from New York City to the Canadian border near Montreal; between Albany and Lake Champlain it closely follows the Champlain Canal.

In addition to the two on-road bike routes, there is a two hundred mile "Canalway Trail" extending across New York. This is a unique off-road network along the Erie, Champlain, Oswego, and Cayuga-Seneca canals. In the future, you'll see more and more of these "Canalway Trails." At present, the system of trails has created many different trail identifications which can be confusing. I've clarified it for you.

Louis Rossi

Typical signage for the Canalway Trail and Bike "5."

- Your second guide is the maps that this book contains, or are available through it.
- Thirdly, you've got me. The signs are not perfect and, alone, are inadequate to get you safely to all important canal sites. There are sections of Bike "5" that you should avoid. Some of the published maps have errors. But I'll pull it all together into a narrative and locate the highlights, tell you where to explore and where to cycle conservatively, and keep you on course.

If you've got the ambition to explore the canals' rich history, this guide will get you where you want to be. This tour is complex with many things to see and many excellent diversions. The Erie Canal is over 300 miles long — the Champlain extends about 60 miles. There are two other operating canals—the Cayuga-Seneca Canal which joins the Erie Canal with the Finger Lakes and the Oswego Canal which links the Erie Canal with Lake Ontario. In addition, there were many other canals, now closed to navigation, that once extended from the Erie Canal north into the Adirondacks and south to New York's Southern Tier. Canal "ruins" are located almost everywhere in the Empire State. These make excellent cycling diversions, too, as communities are opening up their old towpaths for recreational use. I've ridden alongside each canal and will describe them for you. You will find, as I did, that there are numerous opportunities to design your own side trips and diversions.

Louis Rossi

Much of the original towpath is being opened for recreational use.

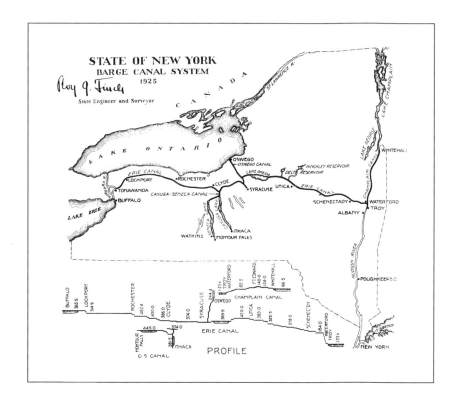

The Barge Canal, built in the 1914, is still a major East-West waterway.

This exploration is possible because much of the original towpath of the 19th century canals is being opened for recreational use. Every year, more and more towpath is opened. Hopes are that someday, there will be a continuous off-road route across New York. Already, over two hundred miles or so of open towpath segments, while not continuous, provide some of the most interesting cycling in America. There are no cars and trucks, no hills to speak of — just the sights and sounds of rural upstate New York.

Today's canals are typically called "Barge Canals;" if you see a sign saying "Barge Canal" it is directing you to the "modern" canal. These "modern," twentieth century canals do not precisely follow the original canal routes. The "modern" Erie Barge Canal, built around 1914, and original Erie Canal closely overlap only in Western New York. Elsewhere, the old Erie was "abandoned" and the newer Barge Canal built, instead, in the parallel river channels. The "modern" Barge Canals, now approaching ninety years of operation, are themselves historic treasures. This tour will search out the best sites of the original canals as well as trace today's barge canals.

I set up this book as a baseline — a way to start cycling through one of the most history-filled regions of the United States. You can start at Albany and ride to Buffalo, or reverse the course. You can pick up a segment at a county line and ride for a day or a few hours. I've suggested a few "canal towns" that can serve as base points for multi-day tours. This guide is arranged to make a complete or partial tour of the entire canal system. For ease, it is really a series of tours that extend, county-by-county, across the Empire State.

Because you are following canals, this is easy riding with few hills. On some tours your ride will be totally flat. However, New York is a very mountainous eastern state. All a cyclist needs to do to find tough hills is to cycle perpendicular to the waterways. There are steep climbs to the north and south of the Mohawk River, south of the canal across central and western New York and close to the Champlain Canal as well. Diversions through these hills are available for the more adventurous. Most often, you'll find quiet, safe, rural roads and scenic vistas that make these detours worthwhile.

Mileage is based on the on-street routes. Milepost zero (MP 0) is at the eastern border of each county for the Bike "5" or Erie Canal route and at the southern border of each county for the Bike "9" or Champlain Canal route. As a county border is crossed, the milepost resets to zero. This arrangement is necessary because there are so many optional visits and detours, that in a short while, no mileage-tracking scheme would remain calibrated. By frequently resetting to zero at county borders, you have repeated opportunities to recalibrate. Starting again at zero, you can easily break the nearly 500 miles of tour route into manageable tours or day trips. This will all be simpler once we get started.

It comes as a surprise to many that the Erie (and other) canals of New York State are living canals. Normally, between May and November, they are open for navigation. Today's canal locks (thirty-five on the Erie, twelve on the Champlain, eight on the Oswego, four on the Cayuga-Seneca), are small parks with ample and safe parking. These make excellent start/stop points for shorter bicycle loops. Typically, canal locks do not have water or other services. Most locks have friendly locktenders who are there to offer you help and advice on any aspect of the canal.

Here are some other items to consider:

- In addition to the maps in this book, there are many locally published maps available to help with your tour. Appendix I lists the major maps you'll want.
- Boat/bicycle trips are possible and currently active boat tour companies are identified in Appendix II.
- Every historic site identified in this itinerary has parking facilities for a day-trip use, and water and bathrooms are usually available. Historic sites are identified in Appendix III. State Historical Sites, operated by the Office of Parks and Recreation, are free of charge. Sites that are privately supported, or federally operated, usually do charge an admission fee.
- You can plan a one-way trip using Amtrak for a return. Rail passenger service extends to all the communities along the Erie and Champlain Canals. However not every train carries bicycles as baggage so check on availability directly with Amtrak.
- Many intercity bus operators will carry your bike as baggage.

Let's discuss the weather. First of all, it gets a bad rap. The weather in upstate New York is really no different from that of the tier of Northeast/Midwest states like Michigan, to the west, or Vermont, New Hampshire, Massachusetts or Maine in New England. Summers are truly wonderful between Memorial Day and Labor Day.

The fall color is just as spectacular as that in New England. Like New England, evenings in the fall can be cool. While winters are long, the canal recreationway remains closed to motorized vehicles and makes an excellent off-road ski trail. Since the canal recreationway lies at a very low elevation, it is often warmer than the hills and mountains to its north or south.

Louis Rossi

Canal locks and their parks are great starting/stopping points.

An Invitation to the Reader

First, a note about the archeology of the canals. About half of the original canals of New York are already open for recreational use — all of the historic original canals lie waiting to be rediscovered. Like buried treasures in Egypt, each year more and more of the original canal infrastructure is being "found" and restored for us to see. As you explore, you'll find an ever-increasing share of American history to enjoy. Often, this is the work of local volunteers or community groups. I recommend you support them with a contribution. Other times, it will be the result of a major funding grant from an agency of the State of New York. Keep your eyes open for more and more canal history to unfold in the future.

Second, an invitation to help us pass on new information on cycling along the canals of New York. Exciting changes are underway with new stretches of towpath are being opened and historic sites being uncovered. If you find that changes have occurred on the routes described in this book, or have new or interesting sites we should add, please let us know so that we can change future editions. The author and the publisher also welcome other comments and suggestions. Address all correspondence to:

Editor
Vitesse Press
 4431 Lehigh Road, #288,
College Park, MD 20740

The Erie and Champlain
Canals in the Capital Region

We've haul'd some barges in our day, Fill'd with lumber, coal and hay, And we know every inch of the way, From Albany to Buffalo.
"The Erie Canal" - American Folk Song

1 / *The Erie and Champlain Canals in the Capital Region*

Civil engineers of the last century were not yet able to control rivers as large as the Hudson or Mohawk so they built the original Erie and Champlain Canals entirely apart from these major rivers. Both the Erie and Champlain Canals left the Hudson River in Albany near the present-day I-90 bridge over the Hudson. Near Green Island, the Erie and Champlain separated paths. The Champlain headed directly north through Cohoes and crossed the Mohawk into Saratoga County near today's Route 32 bridge. The Erie, turning westward, began to climb the Cohoes Falls. Near Crescent, at the Route 9 crossing of the Mohawk River, the Erie, too, crossed over the Mohawk to its north embankment. At Rexford, also known as Aqueduct, the Erie Canal crossed back to the south shore of the Mohawk River. It continued on the south shore all the way west. From Green Island northward, the Champlain followed the Hudson, sometimes on its western shore, sometimes on its eastern. At the beginning of this century, the original Erie Canal was rebuilt as the "Barge Canal" on a new alignment. Today's five Barge Canal locks in Saratoga County (with a lift of about thirty feet each) comprise the highest continuous series of lift locks in the world. I recommend that you visit them. Preserving the old alignments has become an important local objective. Here in the Capital Region, you not only have some the most imposing canal structures, you also have miles and miles of paved Canalway trails.

A "Canalway Trail" extends for more than two hundred miles across New York. In many places, you will see round signs marking four distinct Canalway Trails: Erie, Champlain, Oswego, and Cayuga-Seneca. These represent the State's attempt to bring a unifying "theme" to the dozens of independent efforts that have helped create the off-road trail network that follows these historic canals. In the future, you'll see more and more of these Canalway Trails. However, be alert to the fact that this "bottoms-up" effort to create the system of trails has created many different trail identifications. This can be confusing. You should order a free NYS Canalway Trail Map by calling 1-800-4-CANAL-4.

The Capital Region Around Albany and Schenectady

We are starting (or, if you go west to east, ending) at the most complex part of the journey. Unlike the long stretches of canal that extend east-to-west between Schenectady and Buffalo or north toward Lake Champlain at Whitehall, "navigating" the Canalway Trail in the Capital region of New York State is not simple. There is a lot to see and it takes place in four counties—Albany, Rensselaer, Saratoga, and Schenectady.

Directions To Start

Just a short distance north of downtown Albany, along the Hudson Riverfront, is the Corning Preserve. There is safe daytime parking here and you can pick up the Canalway Trail (called the Corning Trail) right beside the parking area. It is a good place to leave your car for a day trip. If you are looking for secure long-term parking, I would suggest using a nearby hotel garage.

At the Albany waterfront, Bike Routes "5" and "9" and the Canalway Trail overlap. This is the only point where they do so and appropriately marks the start of our trip. If you were going west to

Schenectady in the early 1800s, your choices were: a trip by boat (taking a full day to navigate the twenty-two locks between Albany and Schenectady); one of two turnpikes (the Albany and Schenectady, chartered in 1797, and the Great Western, chartered in 1799); and, after 1831, the Mohawk & Hudson Railroad, the first railroad chartered in America. Today, by bike, you can visit the best bits and pieces of each.

Because of glaciation, Albany is a sea level, fresh-water, Atlantic Ocean seaport; the Hudson River is tidal. In fact, south of Albany, the Hudson is a fjord, one of very few in America. At this point, at the junction of Bike "5," Bike "9," and the Canalway Trail, Henry Hudson ended his voyage of exploration for the "Northwest Passage" almost 400 years ago. The river became too shallow for his ship, the *Half Moon*, to proceed. However, if you look up, on top of the State University administration headquarters, (the former headquarters of the D&H Railroad), the weathervane is a giant replica of the Half Moon. Where Henry Hudson ended his trip, ours begins. This is MP 0 for our bike journey.

Louis Rossi

The Corning Trail at Albany sits on the original basin where the Erie Canal entered the Hudson River. Today it is a pleasant park.

A Special Note on Visiting Downtown Albany

Albany is the second oldest state capital in the United States, settled by the Dutch. Only Santa Fe, settled by the Spanish, is older. A bicycle tour is practical, especially on weekends when urban traffic is light. Worth a visit are three homes where major events in the Revolutionary War and the founding of the American republic were played-out: the Schuyler Mansion (1762), the Ten Broeck Mansion (1798), and Cherry Hill (1763). George Washington, Benjamin Franklin, Benedict Arnold, the Marquis de Lafayette and British General Burgoyne were all visitors of the Schuylers. Alexander Hamilton was married at the Schuyler Mansion.

Visit the New York State Museum at the Empire State Plaza, which is expanding its "Ice Age" exhibits. An ice age mastodont (yes, with a "t"), uncovered near the Cohoes Falls in 1866, is an important part of the exhibit. When I travel, I always find a visit to the State Capitol is an excellent way to learn about a state; the Capitol, in Albany, won't disappoint. The local "Visitors Center" can be found along Bike "9" at Quackenbush Square. Finally, the Albany Institute of History and Art is an excellent museum of local history, especially the Dutch period. In May 1998, the City of Albany holds its Annual Tulip Festival. A bike race in Washington Park is part of this event.

Albany was not the first capital of New York — that was Nieuw Amsterdam, in the Dutch Colony of New Netherlands. In 1664, The English seized New Netherlands and renamed it New York. Nieuw Amsterdam was renamed New York City and remained the colony's capital. However, during the Revolutionary War, the British occupied New York City, and as George Washington fled south, the colonial government fled north. The government ultimately found safety in Albany, where it stayed.

Bike Route "5" is the most direct route to Schenectady. For several miles, you will follow the route of the Great Western Turnpike (NY 20), and the Kings Highway (NY5). It's not the way I recommend, even though it is just nineteen miles. The route is fourteen miles to the Albany/Schenectady County line and five more to downtown Schenectady at the foot of State Street where it crosses the Mohawk River and rejoins the Canal. There is too much traffic and development as well as a lack of historic features. We'll follow the Erie Canal.

Going north from the parking area, right away you face a choice: Bike Route "9" or the first segment of the Canalway Trail (Corning Trail). Both closely follow the route of the original Erie Canal, which is largely invisible today. I recommend the Canalway Trail as it closely follows the Hudson. The path ends, MP 6, in Watervliet. Go under I-787 and take an immediate right onto Broadway in Watervliet. (There is a map on the next page which will show you this route.) In a few short blocks, Bike "9" joins from the left. You will be following Bike "9" through Watervliet and Troy to Waterford.

However, Watervliet contains your first recommended stop, the Watervliet Arsenal (MP 6.5). The Arsenal, founded in 1813, remains the last American manufacturer of cannon. The museum, spanning almost 200 years, is well worth a visit. It contains many historic and interesting buildings and a detailed history of the manufacture of cannon. You shouldn't miss it. And you'll be going right by the main gate on Broadway. You must pass through security, but visitors are welcome. There is no charge.

At Second Avenue (NY Route 32) and Twenty-fifth Street in Colonie (just north of the Watervliet City line), is a small park identifying the site of the eastern "Weighlock" building which once stood here. (When you get to Onondaga County you can see an actual Weighlock.) If you wish to make this short detour, the map on the next page should be helpful.

After leaving the Watervliet Arsenal, at MP 8, Bike "9" turns right and crosses the Hudson River over the Green Island bridge into Troy (Rensselaer County). This is MP 0 in Rensselaer County. This is the recommended route to Waterford.

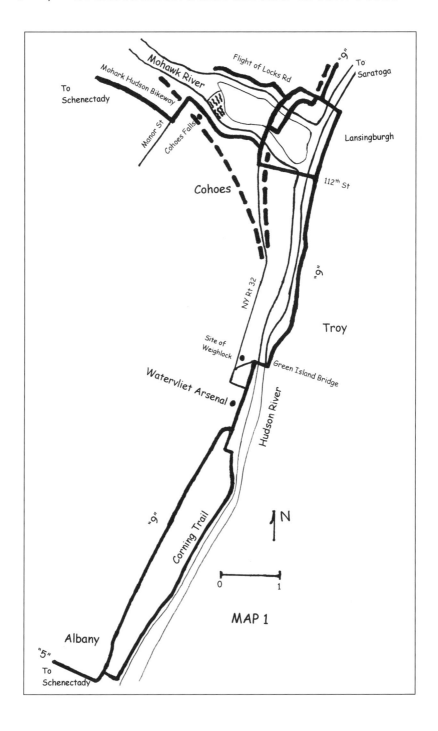

MAP 1

Boat tours on the Hudson and through the flight of locks at Waterford are available in Troy.

In Troy, Bike "9" takes you through several neighborhoods and along the Hudson for four miles. Be careful with traffic in this area as there are several busy intersections. It is hard to find, but you may notice a "Federal Lock" on the Hudson River, in Troy. This lock was not a part of the original canal system, but was built to provide a navigable waterway to Troy, adjusting for fluctuations in the Hudson due to snow melt from the Adirondacks and Catskills and tides from the Atlantic. When the modern barge canals were built, they entered the Hudson River north of Troy and all canal traffic then passed through this "Federal Lock."   This lock now called "Lock One." This explains why the first lock on the Erie Barge Canal is now called "Lock 2."

Louis Rossi

Be sure to stop and talk to the locktender about canal history.

Waterford is your next important destination. It is not hard to find. If you stayed on Bike "9" in Troy, and did not detour at 112th Street, in just one more mile (MP 4), you will cross back across the Hudson River and come into Waterford, which is where you should be. You want to go to the Canal Park, at Canal Lock 2, in Waterford. To get there, if you've arrived in Waterford on Bike Route "9," you need to go straight ahead on Broad Street — do not follow "9" which turns north (right) on 3rd Street. You'll see the sign for Canal Lock 2 on your left after passing through the village center. This little street is hard to find, but do stop to see the exhibits at this site.

Visiting Waterford Canal Sites

The sign welcoming you to Waterford will tell you that it is the oldest incorporated village in America (1794). As Waterford is the eastern hub of today's canal system as well as an important junction on the historic Champlain Canal, plan to spend some time here. Erie Barge Canal Lock 2 has excellent interpretive information on both the old Erie and old Champlain Canals (three old Champlain Canal locks are preserved here), plus excellent information on the "modern" Erie. Talk to the locktender; he'll have a wealth of information. Lock 2 has excellent, safe parking. Also in Waterford, close to the junction of the Erie Canal and the Hudson River, is a historic "canal town." Dozens of small frame houses and narrow streets give this area a unique architectural character. Waterford itself is a pleasant village trying to preserve its canal heritage.

After visiting Waterford, be sure to take the trip up "Flight of Locks Road." It is surely a highlight of any canal tour. This is the highest flight of locks in the world. As you go by Lock 3, look across the Canal. You'll see the Waterford canal shops and dry docks. These shops, not open to the public, are a veritable museum of industrial America. Built "new" in 1914, they continue to make the various pieces of canal paraphernalia that enable the canals to operate today.

At the top of the climb note the twin set of guard gates; these can completely close the canal for protection against damage in the winter and for maintenance. At the top of the flight is a small park and a nice rest stop. See the detail map below.

From Waterford, whether you are going north or west, things get a great deal simpler.

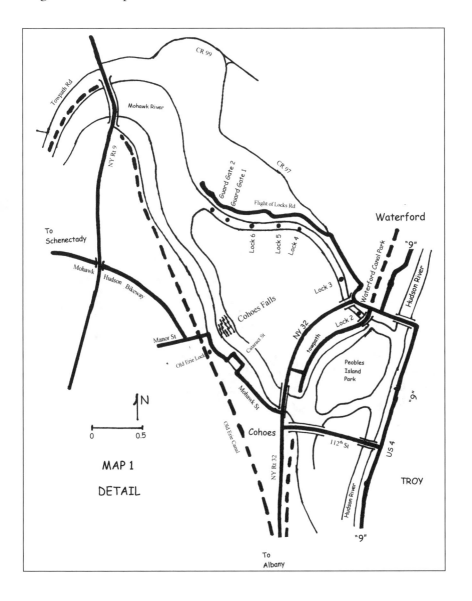

If you are going to follow the Champlain Canal northbound, all you need to do is go back to the center of Waterford and take 3rd Street, which is Bike "9." You'll be following "9" for some fifty more miles to Whitehall. It's really easy to find your way. See Chapter 5.

If you're going to follow the Erie Canal west to Schenectady, there are options shown on the attached map. I recommend going back to Cohoes, picking up the "Mohawk-Hudson Bikeway," and following it along the south shore of the Mohawk into Schenectady. The map shows you where to go. First, be sure to find the old Champlain Canal towpath which extends southward from the park at Lock 2. Walk your bike across the lock gate and you'll easily find the start of this bit of old towpath. I suggest that you carefully look for the Champlain Canalway Trail and pick up an enjoyable, short section of the old Champlain Canal towpath. This bit of out-of-the-way towpath is the only place in the eastern half of New York State to see what the canals of the mid-1800s actually looked like. This section of path is unpaved and ends at Fulton Street in Waterford.

Louis Rossi

The entrance to the old Champlain Canal towpath on Fulton Street.

Fulton Street takes you to NY Route 32; turn left, southward. Cross the Mohawk River and you'll be in Cohoes. Take your first right and climb the hill to the overlook at the Cohoes Falls; this is well signed. Be sure to make this stop.

Louis Rossi

Cohoes Falls in the Spring. The original Erie Canal required eighteen locks to overcome this obstacle.

Schenectady, 230 feet higher than Albany, sits above the 169-foot high Cohoes Falls. These falls were the tallest obstacle that canal builders had to overcome. Originally, in 1825, 18 locks (all in Albany County) were required just to bypass the falls. These are mostly invisible today but some can still be found within Cohoes. These falls were a sacred place to the Mohawk Indians. Indian lore explains that the Mohawk Indian Hiawatha conceived of the Iroquois Confederation while meditating at this spot. Since the Mohawk is the source of water for today's canal locks, the falls can only be seen in full splendor only in the spring. In the autumn after a dry summer, all the water is diverted for canal usage, leaving the falls dry.

The original 15 locks required to climb the Cohoes Falls remain to be rediscovered. Most lie within the City of Cohoes, but are very difficult to find. A sharp eye will pick out the ruins of one lock along the recommended route; it lies just above the Cohoes Falls, on the south side of Mohawk Street, just before the turn up Manor Street.

After seeing the Falls, return to Mohawk Street, turn upriver, westbound, to Manor Street. Go left and uphill. You'll come to the Mohawk-Hudson Bikeway. Turn right, eastbound. After a short unpaved section, pavement resumes. The "Mohawk-Hudson Bikeway" offers a beautiful ride along the Mohawk River, and the Barge Canal. Two town parks, one in Colonie and another in

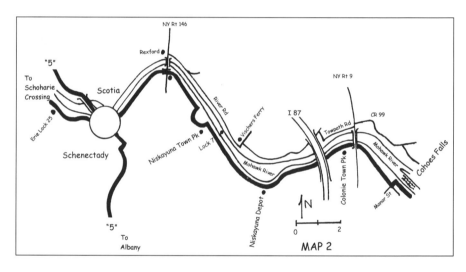

Niskayuna, are open to the public. Also, there is a small park at the old Niskayuna rail depot and at Barge Canal Lock 7. You'll enter Schenectady County along the way. Detailed maps of this bikeway are available from Albany or Schenectady Counties (See the Resource Section for contact information.)

This segment of Canalway Trail is built atop the roadbed of the Troy & Schenectady Railroad (opened in 1842). This railroad was built to connect the first railroad bridge across the Hudson River, at Troy, with the predecessors of the New York Central Railroad at

Schenectady. The plan was to place Troy astride this famous railroad route. However, shortly afterward, the first railroad bridge at Albany was built — the mainline remained through Albany, and this little railroad became a branch line. As you travel westward, you will see the close intertwining of canal history and railroad history.

The Erie Canal did not follow the south shore of the Mohawk River, but crossed to the north shore, near the current Route 9 bridge (Crescent). There are also interesting canal ruins in the pretty village of Vischer's Ferry but these are on the north shore of the Mohawk (see map). These are not on the recommended route, but not difficult to find by bike, should you choose to explore on your own.

Louis Rossi

The Mohawk-Hudson Bikeway at Niskayuna Depot
between Cohoes and Schenectady.

Up ahead, along the Mohawk-Hudson Bikeway, you'll find another small canal park just before Schenectady at Aqueduct/Rexford, (NY Route 146). Here, you can see portions of the Rexford Aqueduct which once carried the original Erie Canal back over and across the Mohawk River to the south shore once again. This was one of the largest aqueducts ever built in New York (610 feet long with 14 arches) and it's definitely worth a stop. This site is a popular spot for canoeists and scullers. There are a number of sculling boathouses and a commercial store, "The Boat House," which rents canoes and offers sculling lessons. You may spot a local race as you cycle past.

Louis Rossi

Scullers training on the Barge Canal near the old Rexford Aqueduct.

As you enter Schenectady, get off the Mohawk-Hudson Bikeway at Nott Street, which passes beneath you. Just off Nott Street are historic neighborhoods — the "Stockade" and the "GE Plot." You must cycle through the "Stockade" and the "GE Plot" is just a short detour. Traffic in these two neighborhoods is generally light.

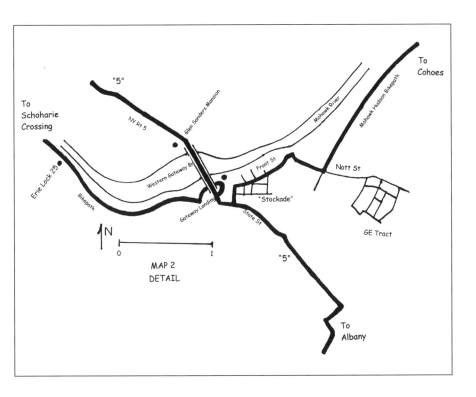

First, visit the "GE Plot." Turn east up Nott Street, go past Union College (a campus dating from 1790), and you'll come to the "GE Plot" in a few short blocks (see above detail map). This small neighborhood was planned by the General Electric Company, whose headquarters was once in Schenectady, as a site for its principal officers. There are many historic homes from the first part of this century.

Take Nott Street west, toward Erie Boulevard to continue the canal tour. Cross Erie Boulevard (yes, this was once the canal bed) and turn onto Front Street. The large factory buildings ahead of and beside you were all once part of the American Locomotive Works, or "ALCO," which was once one of the largest locomotive factories in the world. Front Street passes through the "Stockade." The "Stockade" dates from 1664. This was the original Dutch trading settlement representing the furthest inland point in the Dutch colony of

Nieuw Amsterdam. In 1690, during the French & Indian Wars, it was burned and subsequently rebuilt. The oldest extant house dates from 1692 and there are eight dating from the 1700s. Be sure to see the statue of Lawrence, the Mohawk Indian, who helped the Dutch settlers against the French. Take a few moments and cycle around the streets of the "Stockade." Following Front Street, you'll come to State Street, which is Bike "5." Turn right (west).

In Schenectady, Bike "5" and the Canalway Trail cross at the Western Gateway Bridge at the Mohawk River. This is MP 5 on Bike "5," 15 miles from its start alongside the Hudson River in Albany. The paved Canalway Trail resumes along the south side of the Mohawk and is the recommended route west. Look for the sign "Schenectady County Gateway Landing." Bike "5" crosses the "Western Gateway Bridge" and follows the north shore of the Mohawk River.

While it is not on the recommended route, if you have the time, cross the Bridge into Scotia and stop at the Glen-Sanders House, which is the very first building on your left, going west. It is a very short detour. This home was a "revolution" in its day. Begun in 1655, it was the first home built west of the Mohawk River. The Mansion is a private business offering gourmet food in the original mansion and lodging in a contemporary addition.

Going west from Schenectady, you should be following the Canalway Trail on the south shore of the Mohawk River, For the first time, you'll be bicycling on the original Erie Canal towpath. You'll go past the main GE plant. Today, this is the home of steam turbine production; once it was GE world headquarters. Proceed. You'll see your first old Erie Canal Lock (Lock 25), and your first intact canal aqueduct. This imposing 60-foot long, triple arch aqueduct, over Flat Stone Creek at Rotterdam Kiwanis Park, was a standard design used for most small water crossings on the Erie. The three arches supported the towpath. The canal bed was below in a carefully caulked wooden trough. The Erie Canal had 32 stone aqueducts and you will see many more as you cycle west across New York. The largest was 1137 feet in length (at Crescent, where nothing remains today); the smallest was just 22 feet at Furgeson Creek near Utica (also demolished). In addition there were many stone culverts. You'll see Culvert No. 59 way ahead at Sims Store in Onondaga County, about half way to Buffalo, so there must have been more than one hundred stone culverts in all.

This seven mile segment (paved) of the Canalway Trail ends in Rotterdam Junction (Scrafford Lane). The Village of Rotterdam Junction takes its name from the railroad junction you will cross at Scrafford Lane. This small rail yard marks the westernmost point on the Boston & Maine Railroad. The B&M reached here to connect with the New York West Shore & Buffalo Railroad. (You will learn more about the NYWS&B as you pedal on into Montgomery County.) In Rotterdam Junction, Bike "5" again crosses the Mohawk River (across Erie Canal Lock 9). Follow Bike "5" westward along NY State Route 5S. Along the way, you'll leave Schenectady County (MP 19) and enter Montgomery County (MP 0).

If you want to base yourself in one place, I recommend staying in Schenectady. One day you can ride east to Waterford and return (about 50 miles). With a little planning, you can take the north shore of the Mohawk in one direction, and cycle back on the south shore afterward. The next day, bike west to Schoharie Crossing (in Montgomery County) and return (about 50 miles). Again, cycling along both shores is a safe option as the roads are excellent. In two solid days of cycling you can see most of the canal history in this region.

The Erie Canal in the Mohawk Valley

As a bond of union between the Atlantic and Western States, it may prevent the dismemberment of the American Empire. As an organ of communication between the Hudson, the Mississippi, the St. Lawrence, the Great Lakes of the north and west and their tributary rivers, it will create the greatest inland trade ever witnessed. ... Governor DeWitt Clinton

2 / The Erie Canal in the Mohawk Valley

Throughout the Mohawk Valley, the original Erie Canal was built entirely separate from the river, along its southern shore. The Erie was enlarged three times in the 19th century, deepening its original four-foot depth to nine feet; locks were expanded commensurately. The fourth and last alteration to the canal moved it into the Mohawk River in this century. This meant that much of the original Erie Canal was abandoned. The state park at Fort Hunter (Schoharie Crossing State Historic Site) is the only place where you can see all four phases of canal construction at one location. It is one of the best canal historical sites in the state.

Montgomery County

Reset your odometer to zero as you cross the county border. If you are continuing an east-to-west canal tour, directions are simple for the riding up ahead. For the forty miles across Montgomery County, both Bike "5" and open portions of the Canalway Trail follow the south side of the Mohawk River.

At MP 3, you will pass Erie Barge Canal Lock 10. At MP 4.5, the Canalway Trail resumes. Take this seven mile paved section, built on an old stretch of the New York, West Shore & Buffalo Railroad.

The NYWS&B was financed by Pennsylvania Railroad interests in an attempt to bankrupt the Vanderbilts, who owned the New York Central Railroad. The NYWS&B was completed between New Jersey and Buffalo. Immediately, the Vanderbilts financed the South Pennsylvania Railroad to retaliate against the Pennsylvania group. J. P. Morgan stepped in to make peace between the giants. The completed NYWS&B was "given" to the Vanderbilts and work on the South Pennsylvania was halted. The New York Central System op-

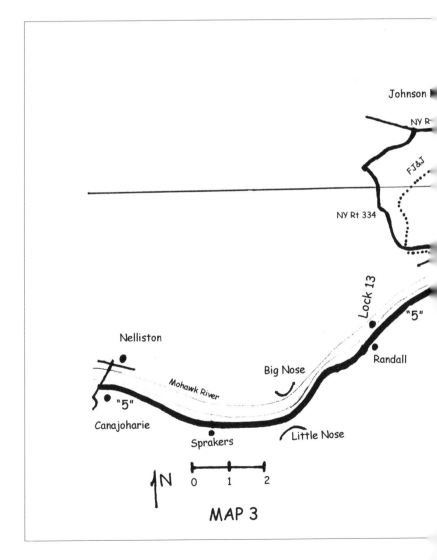

MAP 3

erated the NYWS&B, known locally as the "West Shore," until the 1950s. It may seem hard to believe, but the New York Central was so busy that it needed a total of six tracks between Buffalo and Albany to handle its freight and passenger loadings. After traffic declined in the 1950s, most of the NYWS&B was abandoned in this area.

At Fultonville, definitely see the NYWS&B Freight House. The decorative scrollwork in the eaves still heralds the railroad's original name. At one time, this unique scrollwork design existed at many

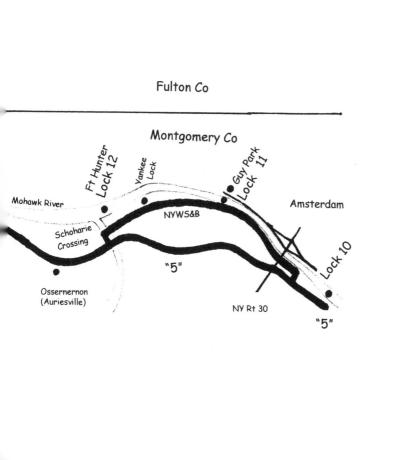

dozens of freight houses which are mostly gone today. As you ride, you will notice the many freight trains moving along the north shore of the Mohawk. These trains are traveling the original New York Central mainline. Between Schenectady and Rochester, the New York Central was built to follow the Erie Canal as closely as possible.

At Amsterdam, cross the Mohawk River and visit Guy Park, the 1773 home of Guy Johnson, and the adjacent Barge Canal Lock 11. This is a pleasant spot for a break. (Another good stop, the home of Guy Johnson's father, Sir William Johnson, is a bit farther west.)

NYS Office of Parks and Recreation/Cliff Oliver Mealy

"Yankee Lock" is one of the best preserved of the old Erie Canal locks.

Take care cycling through Amsterdam and cross back to the south shore as the Canalway Trail continues past Amsterdam, along the south shore of the Mohawk. It will take you directly to two important canal sites: Yankee Lock and Schoharie Crossing, both of which are interesting stopping points.

At Schoharie Crossing, the first historic site on your route is "Yankee Lock" (old Erie Lock #28), which is one of the best preserved of the old locks. Adjacent is Putnam's Store, an authentic canal store. It's two more miles from Yankee Lock to Schoharie Crossing. You can use either the bikepath (paved) or abandoned towpath (unpaved).

NYS Office of Parks and Recreation/Cliff Oliver Mealy

You'll see the largest surviving aqueduct section at Schoharie Crossing.

The Schoharie Crossing State Historic Site is the only place where you'll find all four alignments of the Erie Canal in one place. There is the original "Clinton's Ditch," just four feet deep, and three successive canal enlargements. The largest surviving canal aqueduct is at this site. This was the third largest aqueduct on the Erie Canal and today, about 300 feet of it remains. Just west of the Schoharie Creek, the Canalway Trail ends and rejoins Bike "5." This is MP 11.

The Schoharie Crossing State Park at Fort Hunter makes a good base for day trips. One day, cycle east on the Canalway Trail to Amsterdam, and return either on Bike "5" or the north side of the Mohawk River on Route 5. Another day, bike west on Bike "5" to

Louis Rossi

Bike "5" offers some scenic cycling in the Mohawk Valley.

Fort Plain and return on Route 5. Note that NY Route 5 is a busier highway than NY Route 5S (which is Bike "5"), but it has excellent shoulders and offers a different scenic perspective.

On the hill above where Schoharie Creek and the Mohawk River meet, stood the Mohawk Indian palisaded village of Ossernenon. Known as the "Eastern Door" to the Iroquois Confederacy, this was the principal Mohawk Indian village. (You will see the "Western Door" in Ontario County.) In the 1640s, three French missionaries were killed here; these martyrs became the first American saints. The Auriesville Shrine located here is a major Roman Catholic religious shrine and offers insight into the powerful Iroquois Confederacy.

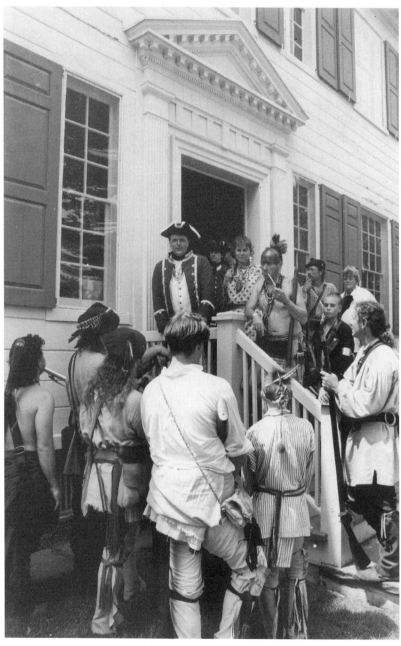

NYS Office of Parks and Recreation/Cliff Oliver Mealy

Plan a side trip to Johnson Hall — one of
the most historic sites in the Mohawk Valley.

Visiting Johnson Hall

If you are interested in the Revolution, you should seriously consider a side trip from Fultonville to see the home of Sir William Johnson. William Johnson was a colonial of immense importance. He successfully fought for the British in the French and Indian Wars, was powerfully allied with the Indians, and was the largest landowner in the valley. In 1763 he built "Johnson Hall," a baronial house and fort. However, the Johnson heirs were Tories in the Revolutionary War and lost everything. Also losers were his ever-faithful Iroquois allies who had followed him in the Tory cause. Today his house is well preserved. Had the British won the war, I am convinced this would be America's "Mount Vernon." This is one of the most significant historical sites in the state.

The site lies north of the Mohawk in Johnstown. The most direct route is to leave Bike "5" at Fultonville (MP 16). Cross the River into Fonda. You now have two choices. You can follow NY Route 30A northward to Johnstown; signs will direct you to Johnson Hall. NY Route 30A has a very steep climb. A slightly longer, and less steep alternative is to follow NY Route 334 to NY 67 and on into Johnstown. It is seven miles from Bike "5" in Fultonville to Johnson Hall via 30A and nine miles between these same end points via the 334/67 route. Take your pick but be sure to visit.

Should you be cycling by in July, you might see one or both days of the Fulton County Road Race. One event is in nearby Gloversville; the other starts and finishes close to Johnson Hall in Johnstown.

Watch for a new bikepath here. Efforts are underway to convert the abandoned Fonda, Johnstown & Gloversville Railroad to recreational use. When this rail trail opens, it will make the preferred bike route between the Mohawk River and Johnstown.

West of Fultonville (actually between the small villages of Randall and Sprakers), the Mohawk River, Erie Canal, and Bike Route "5" pass through the "water-level" gap in the Appalachian chain. This is a geographic feature unique to New York. Nowhere else between Maine and Georgia is there a pass across the Appalachian chain of mountains at this low elevation of 300 feet. Keep in mind that to the north, there are 46 peaks higher than 4,000 feet in the Adirondacks and several that high to the south in the Catskills.

This passageway was the key to much of the history of this region and made the Erie Canal a possibility. In this passage, between "Big Nose" on the north shore, and "Little Nose" on the south shore, all

Louis Rossi

Here, between "Big Nose" and "Little Nose" lies the water-level gap.

that remains of the old Erie Canal are the wetlands you see; the old canal is mostly under the New York State Thruway, which was built over it in the early 1950s.

The Thruway, the first large, divided expressway in America, is the most recent of several centuries of transportation investments in the water-level passage that you see before you.

NYSDOT/Jeff Olson

A tandem heads west toward Fort Plain on Bike "5."

At MP 29, you'll enter Canajoharie, whose library has a surprisingly good collection of American art. Just west of the center of town, the Canalway Trail resumes on an abandoned piece of NYWS&B rail bed. The Canalway Trail will take you three miles on pavement to the pleasant village of Fort Plain. You should visit the site of the Fort (MP 33). Barge Canal Lock 15 is in Fort Plain.

After Fort Plain, Bike "5" leaves the Mohawk River Valley and climbs some small hills. Again, you'll pedal past historic markers noting the remains of Mohawk Indian villages, such as Canawego, at hilltop locations. MP 40 marks the end of Montgomery County.

There is an alternate route that many local cyclists use. For safety reasons, I strongly recommend that you follow Bike "5." However, I want to describe this route because I am sure that in future years, minor bridge repairs will make this a safe cycling route. By following the Mohawk River along River Road, you can avoid the hills, have the opportunity to visit Fort Klock (1750), stay closer to the canal, and see still more historic sites. You will then rejoin Bike "5" in Herkimer County. If you wish to take this detour from Bike "5," look for River Road, westbound, shortly after leaving Fort Plain. Ignore the signs indicating "Dead End" ahead. In just over four miles, you'll come to CR 61 which crosses the Mohawk River into St. Johnsville. I think St. Johnsville is the prettiest of Mohawk Valley villages, and a good place for a rest stop. Fort Klock is just over one mile east of St. Johnsville on NY Route 5. (Jacob Klock was an important leader of Valley Revolutionaries after the death of Herkimer.) After seeing Ft. Klock, reverse your tracks and return to River Road. Back on River Road continuing west, you'll pass Barge Canal Lock 16 and the hamlet of Mindenville. From Mindenville, you can make a very steep climb back to Bike "5" by following Mindenville Road uphill.

Here, River Road crosses the canal onto an artificial island between the Barge Canal and the Mohawk River. Ahead, you'll come to a closed bridge that crosses back across the canal. This bridge is dangerous. The portion that crosses the abandoned NY WS&B railbed has many mission planks and wide gaps that are hazardous to cross. You must dismount and walk your bike across — and you should be comfortable with heights! After the bridge, River Road resumes and rejoins Bike "5," NY 5S, in Herkimer County near the Herkimer Home. Because River Road is no longer a through road for vehicular traffic, it makes for an excellent bike ride. Be careful if you are traveling eastbound. Shortly after leaving the Herkimer Home, you'll see River Road on your left. Again, ignore the "Dead End" sign and be very careful at the bridge. You can follow River Road all the way to Fort Plain.

As I mentioned previously, I believe that the bridge will be repaired making this a safe cycling route. For now, I recommend avoiding the bridge and staying on Bike "5" along NY Route 5S.

Herkimer County

Reset your odometer as you enter Herkimer County on Bike "5" or on River Road.

You'll soon come to signs pointing you to the Herkimer Home State Historic Site. I suggest that you stop there. The Herkimer House is 4.5 miles from the border with Montgomery County. Turn off Bike "5" and onto NY 169. (Bike "5" continues westward up a very steep hill along NY Route 5S.) Immediately, you'll see the entrance to the Herkimer Home.

NYS Office of Parks and Recreation/Central Region

The Herkimer Home. No tour of the Mohawk Valley would be complete without stopping here.

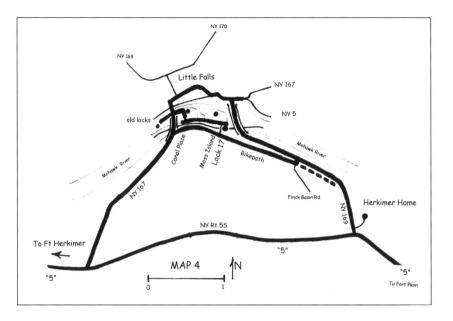

The Herkimers, of German descent, fought against the British in the Revolution. Nicholas Herkimer, an extremely prosperous, slaveowning farmer and trader, built this remarkable home in 1764. Although successful as a farmer, Herkimer made his fortune by using his slaves to haul small boats overland around the Little Falls. In 1777, he left his home to help defeat a major British invading force and lost his life in the effort at the Battle of Oriskany. The house is extremely well preserved and a fascinating counterpoint to Johnson Hall. Almost identical in age, they are quite different, although both are grand. They are truly remarkable, serving as both frontier "mansions" and "forts" simultaneously. As loyalists to the Revolution, the Herkimer family remained in possession of the farm for many years. You might want to rent the old Henry Fonda, Claudette Colbert movie "Drums Along the Mohawk" as good preparation for this visit, in which Roger Imhoff portrays General Herkimer. Better still, for more detail read the recently reprinted book, Drums Along the Mohawk by Walter Edmonds. Edmonds also authored Rome Haul and Erie Water.

Herkimer was a great American hero and should be better re-membered. The Battle of Oriskany was crucial in defeating the west-ern prong of the British plan to capture Albany and sever the colo-nies. Thwarting the British descent of the Mohawk was just as cru-cial as turning back the British descent from Lake Champlain at Saratoga in the same year. The Oriskany Battlefield site lies up ahead.

After leaving the Herkimer home, stay on NY 169 and head to-ward Little Falls, another Erie Canal gem. Plan to spend a little time here — there is a lot of canal history in and around the village. Little Falls got its name because it was the smaller of the two waterfalls along the Mohawk River. As noted before, the Herkimers made their fortune utilizing slaves to haul riverboats around these falls.

Louis Rossi Photo

Beyond the old lock in the foreground, you can spot imposing Lock 17.

As you bike toward town along NY Route 169, you'll come to Barge Canal Lock 17. Be sure to stop. An imposing structure, Lock 17 remains the highest single lift-lock in the world. A smaller lock from the old Erie is nearby for comparison. In all, the old Erie Canal employed four locks to rise above (or descend) these falls. (These were not much larger than those of the earlier private company, which you can see later on.)

There are some glacial potholes at Lock 17 located on Moss Island that certainly justify a rest stop. Glacial potholes are formed at the edge of glaciers, where large rocks are set spinning at the base of icy waterfalls. These twirling rocks actually dig potholes in the base rock. The potholes at Little Falls are numerous and some of the largest in America. Carry your bike up the flight of metal steps to the top of the lock; you'll see a map showing hiking directions. It is only a short distance, but cannot be hiked in cycling shoes with cleats. The walk climbs steeply up over rocks with few handholds. Ask the locktender for directions if you are unsure.

Louis Rossi Photo

The glacial potholes on Moss Island, near
Lock 17, are some of the largest in America.

Now, cycle west less than a mile on the paved service road along the Barge Canal to Little Falls. You'll arrive at Benton's Landing near Canal Place. You'll find still more historic markers and sites describing the complex canal history at this point.

Here, in 1795, a private company, the Western Inland Navigation Company, completed a series of small locks to bypass the Falls. Archeological excavations have unearthed old lock and canal sites just west of Canal Place along Elizabeth Street. General Philip Schuyler, whose home you might have seen in Albany, was a founder of the company that built this small canal.

Louis Rossi

General Philip Schuyler was first president of the Western Inland Navigation Company in 1792.

Also in Little Falls, you will see the main line of the old New York Central again. Still one of the busiest railroads in America, the New York Central emerged from a series of smaller short rail lines in 1851. At Little Falls, the railroad was built as the Utica & Schenectady, opening in 1836. If you follow NY Route 169 across the Mohawk River into Little Falls, there is a small historic marker identifying the site of one of the worst train wrecks on the New York Central Railroad. Here, in 1940, the Lake Shore Limited was derailed at a sharp curve, killing 31 passengers. The curve was later straightened.

As you can tell, there is a lot to see in this small area. Additionally, a short paved railtrail (over the NYWS&B) begins at Finks Basin Road, runs right beside Lock 17, and continues to NY 167. Take a careful look at the map on page 45. It is hard to show everything, but since everything is in a small area, you will find your way easily.

Little Falls is typical of most Mohawk Valley communities — it struggles against the economic decline that began shortly after World War II. However, the village is doing a great job to celebrate its rich canal heritage and in turn, to revitalize the downtown area.

After Little Falls, continue the canal tour westward, looking for signs directing you to NY Route 167. It is a bit complex as the roadway system in Little Falls is way overscaled for traffic needs. However, the system of roads is reasonably "friendly" toward cyclists. NY Route 167 will rejoin NY 5S (Bike "5") in just a few miles.

There are still a few important things to see before leaving Herkimer County. Two miles along on Bike "5" is Lock 18 at Johnsonburg. Its well-marked entrance looks like a driveway, which it is, but try it and you'll come alongside the old Erie Canal again as the access road rides on top of the old towpath. After visiting this lock, less than two miles further is a very important historic site directly alongside Bike "5." This is the Fort Herkimer Church built in 1730. This is the original Herkimer family homestead and site of General Herkimer's birth. The stone church served as a fortress in conjunction with the actual wooden fort which was just a few hundred feet further west.

The site of that fort is now a small roadside park alongside the Mohawk River. To me, this stone church conveys a strong sense of how life was in pre-Revolutionary, frontier America.

Continue west past the villages of Herkimer, Mohawk, and Ilion. Bike "5" bypasses each of them, but feel free to explore them if you have time. The Remington Firearms Museum at Ilion, just off Bike "5," might be of interest to you. Ilion is the home of Remington Arms, and the museum chronicles the history of the firm, which has been at this site since 1816.

At Route 51, Bike "5" turns north and crosses the Mohawk River and turns west onto NY Route 5. Be sure you make this crossing. Follow the signs toward Utica. (Note that the New York State Canalway Trail Map is in error as it shows Bike "5" continuing west on the south shore of the Mohawk.) Following Bike "5" correctly, on the north shore, you'll cycle for a while right alongside the old New York Central mainline. Look for Lock 19 (on your left, westbound, at MP 14) as it is a nice picnic or rest area. Notice how the railroad crosses almost directly in front of the lock. Back on Bike "5," it is just four more miles to the end of Herkimer county.

If you were to cycle directly across Herkimer County on Bike "5," it would be a fast, 26-mile ride. Following the many detours I've recommended will lengthen your trip accordingly.

Eastern Oneida County—to the headwaters of the Mohawk

Bike "5" follows the north shore of the Mohawk River in Oneida County. Be sure to reset your odometer to zero.

At the Oneida County border, you will be on Herkimer Street on the north side of the City of Utica. Utica, unlike the cities to the east such as Schenectady, Troy and Albany, owes its development to the completion of the Erie Canal. This is much the same for Syracuse, Rochester, and Buffalo, all of which grew rapidly as a result of the canal. As such, Utica was not an important site in the wars of the

18th and 19th centuries. A small earthen and wood fort, called Fort Schuyler, was built in 1758 just east of today's Amtrak station. Unfortunately, nothing remains.

A Special Note On Visiting Utica

While Utica is not on the recommended tour, the city does offer some interesting sites. To visit, you need to leave Bike "5." Take either Genesee Street (which is a busy arterial) at MP 2, or a short segment of exclusive bikeway located at MP 4. The bikeway will take you along the Erie Barge Canal to Utica's Barge Canal docks. These are worth seeing because, at one time, every inland city along the Barge Canal had a terminal like this. Remember that these docks linked these small places with the cities of the Great Lakes and Atlantic Seaboard.

You'll have to look carefully for the entrance to the bikeway. It is at MP 4 adjacent to a highway off ramp, across from Flanagan Road. The bike path ends on Genesee Street so you will have to ride the busy street into downtown.

The Amtrak Station is unique in that it is the only one of the few great urban terminals of the New York Central to be preserved and used. It is in excellent condition and contains a bookstore with many books of interest to the transportation historian. Further along (south) Genesee Street are the Munson-Williams-Proctor Institute and the Oneida County Museum. Along Memorial Parkway are a number of statues of famous people. Two are from the American Revolution: General Wilhelm Baron Von Steuben and Brigadier General Casimir Pulaski. None of the original Erie Canal remains to be seen in Utica today. It all lies beneath modern highways.

A very important feeder canal, known as the Chenango Canal, extended almost 100 miles from Utica to Binghamton. It closed in 1878 and remains to be re-opened for recreational use. A five-mile stretch is open between Bouckville and Solsville in Madison County.

The British invasion
of the Mohawk Valley
was turned back here
at the Battle of
Oriskany.

NYS Office of Parks and Recreation/Central Region

Whether you detour at Utica or not, you should head west on Bike "5." Be aware that going west, Bike "5" becomes a limited access highway just west of Utica. The shoulders on NY Route 49 are wide and the frequent Bike "5" signs reassure you that you are on track. This road makes fine, fast cycling, but be forewarned — there are no services along this stretch of road.

I recommend that you divert from Bike "5" to see an important Revolutionary War site on the south side of the river at Oriskany. Leave Bike "5" at the "Oriskany" off-ramp. From here, it is three miles to the battlefield. Directional signing is poor, but all you have to do is cross over the Mohawk and turn west on NY 69, which will take you directly to the site.

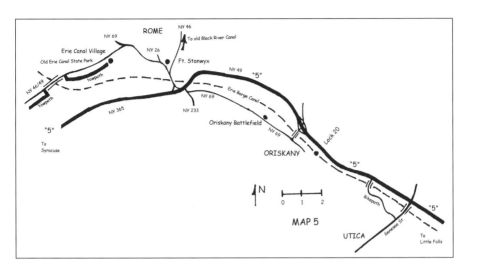

The Oriskany Battlefield Historical Site is the location of one of the most important battles of the Revolution. It was here that the British invasion of the Mohawk Valley was turned back, and plans to link up with the invading force under General Burgoyne thwarted. Here, General Herkimer was mortally wounded. Reenactments take place every August 6th.

After your visit, do not retrace your steps. Instead, continue west on NY 69 until it joins NY 365. Here Bike "5" signs resume. Once again, we are going to leave Bike "5" up ahead at the interchange with State Routes 69/49/26 and head northwest into the City of Rome. This will bring you to Fort Stanwix and, in turn, Erie Canal Village, which will open up 36 miles of great riding on the Old Erie Canal State Park towpath. Route 26 will take you into Rome and to Fort Stanwix — be careful with the traffic along this short stretch.

Downtown Rome was "modernized" with major urban renewal so the rebuilt Fort Stanwix sits there as a historic island in a sea of cars and highways. Fort Stanwix marks the western end of the Mohawk River. From here it was a short portage of only one mile to the Wood Creek, which extended into Oneida Lake and on to Lake Ontario. This ancient path, used by Indians for centuries, was an important strategic route during the Revolutionary War. Fort Stanwix, originally built in 1758, choked off access from Lake Ontario. The successful defense of this fort prevented the British from entering the Mohawk River Valley. Had they been able to do so, the possibility of a successful link-up with General Burgoyne's troops moving south down the Champlain Valley toward Saratoga was very real. The victory at Fort Stanwix along with the defeat of the British at Saratoga, were the turning points in the Revolutionary War.

Although from a military perspective the American Revolution in the Mohawk Valley was a success, the population fared poorly from the almost constant warfare. According to historians, less than a third of the population remained after the "successful" conclusion of the many wars in the valley. Many were dead. Many settlers were Tories who fled for their lives. The power of the Iroquois Confederation, which had joined the British side, was broken forever.

To continue, pedal west on Route 46. From Fort Stanwix, signs leading you to Erie Canal Village are quite easy to follow. However, the streets are busy — avoid them at peak traffic periods.

A Note on the Classical Names in Upstate New York

You have now cycled through Ilion, Utica, and Rome. The Black River Canal extended from Rome to Carthage. Continuing west, you will pass through Verona, Mycenae, Manlius, Syracuse, Galen, Cato, Greece, Egypt, Macedon, Medina and other place names from the classical world. Why? The answer to this mystery arises out of the many wars which took place in upstate New York. Constant warfare with the Indians and between the British and French kept colonial New York limited to the Hudson Valley and a few parts of the eastern Mohawk Valley. Opening the territory west of Rome for safe settlement coincided with the founding of the American republic. With an exuberance that befit both events, people in the late 1700s used names from classical Rome and Greece to indicate the promise they saw in their new communities and the new Republic.

A Diversion — The Black River Canal

There's a scenic segment of the Black River Canal north of Rome. Back before the Erie Canal was even finished, Governor DeWitt Clinton began looking for more water to keep his "ditch" filled. He recommended tapping the Black River and, after years of surveys and hassles, construction began in 1836. The canal began carrying water to Rome in 1849 and opened to boat traffic in the next year. It served as the major link for moving lumber and other goods for 75 years until abandoned in 1922. Driving north to Boonville on Route 46 you can see vestiges of the old canal. You can see more locks heading north from Boonville on Route 12 toward Lyons Falls.

Dick Mansfield

Take your hybrid or mountain bike to
the Black River Canal towpath trail.

A local group, with help from the state and communities, has established a trail along the old towpath. The trail, closed to motorized vehicles, is groomed for cross-country skiing in the winter and used by hikers in the summer. It is a great bike ride for the whole family since it is smooth riding with very little climbing. The towpath is smooth and level with short climbs each time you come to a lock. Brush and trees cover many of the locks but it's easy to spot where they are located — because you will come to another brief rise in the towpath. (The canal had 109 locks over its 35-mile length.) This is an out and back trip of 15 miles.

From Rome, take Route 46 north for 17 miles. The parking area is on the right 4.5 miles past the hamlet of North Western, just after you pass the Town of Ava sign. Look for the sign.

The Erie Canal in Central New York

The bicycle shall be the greatest single emancipator of women.
Susan B. Anthony

3 / The Erie Canal in Central New York

Fort Stanwix guards the western headwaters of the Mohawk River; from here, the Mohawk River bends northwards into the Adirondacks. As you bike westward, you will cross some of New York's flattest topography. This made building the Erie Canal easier, but it also meant crossing New York's worst swamplands. This lowland is the bottom of an ancient glacial lake called Lake Iroquois. The southern shores of that lake are the hilltops you see to your south. Lake Iroquois was so big, extending over much of the Eastern Great Lakes that in relation, today's giant Lake Ontario is a mere puddle. When the ice cap melted enough to permit the waters of Lake Iroquois to spill out, the resultant flood was so instantaneous and large that it altered the drainage pattern of Eastern North America. No longer would the Great Lakes drain southward through the Mississippi River but northeast into the Saint Lawrence. Today, in terms of volume of water flow, the Saint Lawrence remains the largest river in North America.

The longest, unspoiled sections of the original Erie Canal unfold in Central New York. This is because the builders chose an entirely new alignment when they built the modern Erie Barge Canal here early in the century. The present Barge Canal system uses Oneida Lake and the Oneida and Seneca Rivers to extend westward. The old canal alignment lies well south. Because today's canal is so separate from the historic canal, this portion of our tour lets us see the Erie Canal as it was in the 19th century, for the most part, unchanged.

Western Oneida and Madison Counties

For the day-tripper, the Erie Canal State Park, which stretches from Rome to Syracuse, provides a unique cycling opportunity. This unspoiled section of original Erie Canal is its own "tour" extending over thirty miles. We have reprinted excerpts from the map of this section — see the Resource Guide for ordering information.

Here's a surprise. If you have been riding along the Erie Canal since Albany you are, just now, arriving at the Canal's starting point. From a canal perspective, it is important to note that it all began here, on July 4, 1817, when the digging began near Rome.

Why here? This was not an easy place to reach in those days. Using the old politician's trick, still very much in use today, Governor Clinton did not begin digging his "ditch" from one or both ends; he began in the middle. Of course, getting started in the middle, then, as now, meant that you had to complete everything to have a useful canal. Unless the entire canal was finished, the middle sections would prove useless. Moreover, as the middle sections were the most level (flattest), more work could be accomplished quickly.

This section, called the "Long Level," is unique in that it had no locks for over fifty miles. The original Erie Canal builders achieved a totally flat alignment between Lock 46 just west of Utica, and Lock 47 in Syracuse. Builders of today's Erie Barge Canal achieved an even longer "Long Level"— you'll see that stretch further west. Remarkably, this oldest section of Erie Canal, though closed to commercial boat traffic, is still in use. It brings water from reservoirs located south of Syracuse to the "summit" of the Erie Barge Canal west of Rome. You can still, in season, catch a mule-towed canal boat ride from the Erie Canal Village.

To proceed west from Rome, get on the old towpath which begins at Erie Canal Village. It is an easy ride on mostly unpaved stone dust path for the thirty-six miles to Syracuse. While there are no locks, there are three well-preserved old aqueducts, still carrying water to the summit of today's Barge Canal.

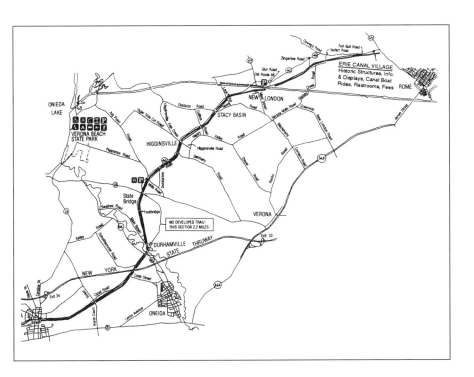

About ten miles into the ride, near State Bridge, you will ride one section on the road. Bike "5" intersects and continues west, along State Route 31 across Madison County. Unless you are in a hurry, don't use Bike "5." Instead, follow the Erie Canal State Park trail. While the thirteen mile trip across Madison County on this section of Bike "5" (NY Route 31) makes for fast riding and takes you along Oneida Lake, you'll miss too much of the grand old Erie.

Along the way, there are some interesting stopping points. In Canastota, you'll find a small canal museum. South of Canastota, on County Route 25, at Nichols Pond Park, is the site of an Oneida Indian village attacked by Samuel de Champlain in 1615. The Indians prevailed that time.

About five miles further, in Chittenango, you'll find the restored old canal dry docks at the Chittenango Landing Canal Boat Museum. There is an interpretive center, the dry docks, and a sawmill-blacksmith complex. Also in Chittenango is the home of L. Frank

Baum, author of "the Wizard of Oz." Chittenango has yellow brick sidewalks and an "Oz Festival" each May. Baum's birthplace is on State Route 13, south of the Village. Without question, the builders of the Erie Canal, like the Tin-man, Scarecrow and Lion, had "heart, brains, and courage."

If you find the lack of pavement along the towpath to be troublesome, excellent low-volume local roads follow the old canal bed very closely. With a little road savvy you will have a very enjoyable trip and miss none of the important stops along the way. If you wander at all, you will come to the nearby tracks of the New York Central — built as the Utica & Syracuse Railroad.

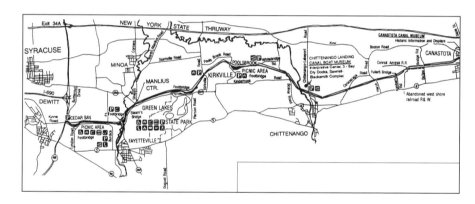

Onondaga County

Still on the old towpath, you'll find several other nice stopping points along the way. Just beyond Chittenango, you'll enter Onondaga County and come upon the Poolsbrook Picnic Area, where there are restrooms and parking.

Further ahead, just to the south of the canal, is the beautiful Green Lakes State Park complete with bathing beach and camping areas. The "Green Lakes" are also significant glacial features. There are two lakes, two hundred feet deep, with a unique aquamarine color. Round Lake is a National Natural Landmark. It is a "plunge pool," something like a giant "pothole." If the potholes you saw on Moss Island were big enough for a few people to stand in, these two plunge pools are small lakes. They are formed in much the same way. Be sure to climb to the top of the park's access road, above the golf course, to see the higher, unspoiled lake.

Continuing west from Green Lakes, just before crossing the Limestone Creek aqueduct, you'll see a small canal bed and towpath heading off to the south. This is a short stretch of old feeder canal that once connected the Village of Fayetteville with the Erie Canal. If you have been traveling all the way from Rome and are looking for food or a place to stay before heading into Syracuse, you might try Fayetteville. The old feeder canal towpath will lead you right to the village center. This stretch of feeder canal is typical of many built to connect the old Erie Canal with small villages just off its course.

Louis Rossi

Butternut Creek Aqueduct, east of Syracuse, is typical of smaller Erie Canal aqueducts. Note how the original towpath now carries the Erie Canalway Trail.

The Old Erie Canal Park Trail ends at the Cedar Bay Picnic Area in Dewitt, a few miles west of Fayetteville, and just outside the City of Syracuse. As in most upstate cities, the Erie Canal lies under modern highways. You have two options for proceeding: return to Bike "5" or use busy local city streets.

It is simple to get back to Bike "5" from the western end of Erie Canal State Park. Simply take any one of a number of quiet north-south local roads on the eastern side of Onondaga County that link the two; you will not get lost. I recommend Kirkville Road. Once back on Bike "5," follow it as it circles around the north side of Syracuse until it rejoins the Canalway Trail near Jordan. Sections of it are busy, but it is the best choice.

If you choose to follow Bike "5," it is 33 miles all the way across Onondaga County. In Onondaga County, Bike "5" more closely follows the route of the Barge Canal. At MP 16, Belgium, and at MP 18, Baldwinsville, you will again cross over the Erie Barge Canal. The map below explains possible route options.

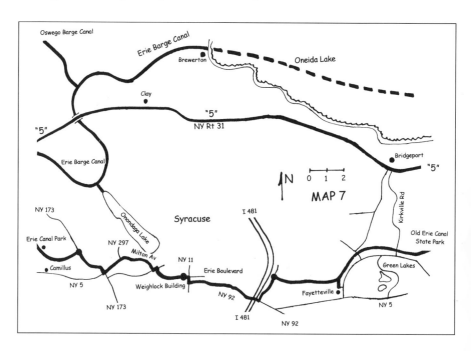

A Special Note on Visiting Syracuse

Downtown Syracuse contains the Erie Canal Museum which is located in an old "weighlock building," built in 1850. While once there were seven, it survives as the only weighlock. A weighlock is exactly what it seems — a place where canalboats are weighed and tolls collected. Tolls collected from the Erie Canal once paid the entire budget of the State of New York. An especially fascinating aspect of this building is the means of weighing the canalboats. Originally, when first opened, the simplest of all means was used. As the boat entered the lock, locktenders measured the volume of water it displaced. As the weight of water is a known constant (62.4 pounds per cubic foot), the amount of water displaced gave the weight of the boat through simple multiplication. The ancient Greeks knew this — it is called Archimedes Principle. (Archimedes was a citizen of the ancient Greek colony of Syracuse, located in today's Sicily.) Well, no self-respecting canal boat captain of the 1830s was going to believe any of that. Having just as much confidence in the government tax collector as we do today, boaters insisted, and got, replacement of the original system with a complete system of cradles and scales. Until tolls were removed, boats would be weighed by draining the weighlock, allowing the boats to settle dry onto cradles, and using "official weights" on scale beams.

Visiting the Canal Museum is worthwhile and will give you an excellent perspective on how the old Erie Canal shaped a major American city which was built astride it. It has an excellent bookstore for canal buffs. It lies between Water Street and Erie Boulevard, behind City Hall. Erie Boulevard is a busy roadway built on top of the original canal bed. Therefore, getting to the Weighlock Building by bicycle is best left to off-peak travel periods. Since the old Erie Canal Towpath ends east of the city (in Dewitt) and resumes west of the city (in Camillus), and Bike "5" is circling north of the city on NY Route 31, an adventurous cyclist must make his or her way downtown over busy Syracuse streets. No route is really attractive. To reach the museum from the end of the Canal Park in Dewitt, take Butternut Drive to Genesee Street (Route 5 and 92) and follow Genesee Street (NY Route 92) six miles from Dewitt to downtown. Traveling from west to east, it is difficult to make the left from Genesee onto Butternut (look for Pickwick) — the street is hard to find, the left turn is hazardous, and it is located in a busy interchange.

Louis Rossi

The Weighlock Building in Syracuse holds the Erie Canal Museum.

Once in Syracuse, you'll find it has a very attractive downtown. Just a few blocks west of the Canal Museum (Weighlock Building) is Clinton Square. This was once the "harbor" of Syracuse, and the junction of the Erie and Oswego Canals. Pictures in the Canal Museum will show you what this site once looked like. Of course, no one can replicate what it must have smelled like. In its heyday, jammed with horses and mules, with the canal itself serving as the toilet for canalboat passengers and crew, one can only imagine. Syracuse has plans to return this space to pedestrian use; it will be a beautiful spot when it does. There is a lot of interesting architecture awaiting you in Syracuse. Like all cities, however, its busy weekday streets call for touring by bicycle on the weekend.

We have reached the geographic center of New York. Syracuse lies mid-point between Albany and Buffalo. The Iroquois Confederation was governed from hilltops to the south of today's city. The Onondaga were the central tribe in the Iroquois Confederacy. Their great "longhouse" still exists on a reservation south of Syracuse where the "Council Fire" is maintained. As we earlier learned, the Mohawk village of Ossernenon was the "Eastern Door" of the Confederacy. The Seneca settlement at Ganondogan was the "Western Door." Here, on Onondaga lands was the location of the "Council Fire" of a symbolic "Great Longhouse" that extended for several hundred miles across what is now New York. This symbolism was important in uniting the five nations. With canoes and natural waterways, the Confederacy governed an "Indian Empire" extending about 150 miles to the east and west of this point. These Indians, collectively, called themselves the Haudenosaunee, or "People of the Longhouse." The French used the word "Iroquois." The British referred to these Indians as the Five Nations.

After visiting the Erie Canal Museum and downtown Syracuse, follow Erie Boulevard westward (you are on top of the old canal) from downtown. At the intersection with West Genesee Street, turn westward; almost immediately, turn right onto Milton Avenue. As you leave Syracuse, you'll enter the Town of Geddes. The town is named after James Geddes, who, more than anyone, is responsible for selecting the route of the Erie Canal across Western New York. You will learn more about his work in Monroe County. You will come alongside the old Auburn & Syracuse Railroad, another rail link in the first chain of railroads that crossed New York. Route 297 will join Milton Avenue; continue straight. You will enter the Town of Camillus. At the intersection of NY Route 173, turn right. In 1.5 miles you will come to the Erie Canalway trailhead. It will be on your left. Look for a small sign "Town of Camillus Erie Canal Park." If you come to Reed Webster Park, you've gone a bit too far.

A Diversion — The Oswego Canal

The Oswego Barge Canal diverges from today's Erie Barge Canal north of Syracuse. The old Oswego Canal once began right in downtown Syracuse, at Clinton Square, near the Weighlock Building, and like all the canals of that time, was entirely separate from the natural riverbeds. Today's Oswego Canal extends north from the modern Erie Canal and for its full extent utilizes the Oswego River. (Should you wish to make the lengthy side trip, Fort Ontario, built in 1755, at Oswego, is still another very well preserved stone fort. It changed hands many times in its history. After World War II, European Jews who had been freed from concentration camps, were temporarily housed here, although denied official entry into the United States.) Oswego hosts a "HarborFest" each July. On the way, you'll pass through Fulton, home of Nestle's. It hosts a "Chocolate Festival" each summer. A recreation path (rough and unpaved) extends east from Fulton to Cleveland on Oneida Lake. The trail lies on the abandoned roadbed of the New York, Ontario & Western Railway.

Also, Oswego lies about the mid-point of the 454-mile "Seaway Trail" which extends from the Canadian border, near Rooseveltown, along Lakes Ontario and Erie to the Pennsylvania Border near Ripley. The "Seaway Trail" is clearly beyond the scope of this guide; you can obtain information by calling the 800-number in the Reference Guide. A cyclist should be aware that the Seaway Trail is laid out with auto travel in mind — some Seaway Trail roads are excellent for cycling; others are dangerous. A cyclists' guide is available.

There are so many ways of cycling up to Lake Ontario that I am not making a recommendation. Take care in choosing an on-road route — you would be wise to contact a local cycling club or bike shop for recommendations. It is possible to make an extensive loop trip that will take you through Oswego, west to Fair Haven (a glacial estuary) along the Seaway Trail, then back to the Erie Canal in Cayuga County via a rail trail. See the text and map on Cayuga County.

At Camillus, you are now back on the original Erie Canal tow-path. This section of path extends from Camillus across Onondaga and Cayuga counties. However, unlike the section of towpath on the eastern side of Syracuse which is a park under state jurisdiction, this 18-mile stretch is locally owned and maintained by volunteers.

After a short ride west, you will come to Sims Store. This was not only a general store and departure station for persons riding canalboats, but also a residence of John Sims and family. Local lore has it that baby Susie's carriage rolled into the canal with Susie aboard, perhaps persuading John to move his family elsewhere. Today, there are many Sims descendants in the Camillus area. You'll find many excellent interpretive signs to help explain canal history at this site. It is easy to visualize canalboats plying this section of Erie Canal. Perhaps no section of the old canal has been restored better than that in Camillus. Hundreds of volunteers have cleared the canalbed, built dams and filled the canal with water. Conditions vary depending on the energy of local volunteer groups. Canalboat tours run on Sundays from May to October.

Dick Mansfield

Sims Store in Camillus lies along a restored section of canal.

Excellent directional signs near Jordan. The Canalway Trail is on your left while Bike "5" continues westward.

Louis Rossi

Local signage near Peru.

Heading west, conditions on the towpath vary greatly. In the spring-time, it might be muddy. However, excellent paved local roads run parallel to the canal in this area and it is not difficult to follow the old canal by road. At Warners, the old towpath is open for vehicles and the canalbed is clogged with debris. Persevere. The canal path continues through Memphis to Peru. Here, you'll need to jog around some private homes to pick up the towpath once again. There is an interesting aqueduct and waste weir at Peru. Then it is on to Jordan, which is the first large town heading west. This is a good place to "refuel." You'll rejoin Bike "5" in Jordan, at the western edge of Onondaga County.

Cayuga and Seneca Counties

Following Bike "5" it is 12 miles across Cayuga County and one mile across Seneca County. The Erie Canalway Trail (local signs say "Cayuga County Trail") extends all the way across Cayuga County. Trail conditions vary, but the good news is that Bike "5" is almost directly adjacent to the old canal and offers a continuous, safe on-road alternative. Once again, there is a lot to see. The names themselves: Weedsport, Centerport and Port Byron, all in the space of five miles, speak to us. What were "ports" doing in Central New York? As construction of the Canal progressed west of Syracuse, new territory was being opened. No longer was the "modern" canal transportation linking up old villages. Now, for the first time, new places were springing up along the expanding canal. These promising sites were major "ports" in their day. At Centerport, be sure to see the Centerport Aqueduct Historic Site; it is on the Cayuga County Trail and directly adjacent to Bike "5" on the south side.

The "Cayuga County Trail" is a nice diversion, but don't expect to find facilities in as good condition as those in the Erie Canal State Park. Be prepared to explore a little. A trick is to look for street names like Dock Street, Lock Street, Towpath Road, Water Street, Erie Street or Erie Boulevard, and so forth. These are often access points to old canal sites. A test for the skillful canal explorer is to try to find the ruins of the Seneca River Aqueduct. This aqueduct was 840 feet long with 31 stone arches. Hint: It is near the village of Montezuma.

While I find the Cayuga County Trail a little hard to follow, and conditions a little too difficult for narrow high-pressure tires, it is worth trying. Although the trail is really intended for horses and snowmobiles, it is easy to follow the towpath by adjacent paved road, and you won't get lost. Remember, Bike "5" is always alongside to redirect you safely back on course.

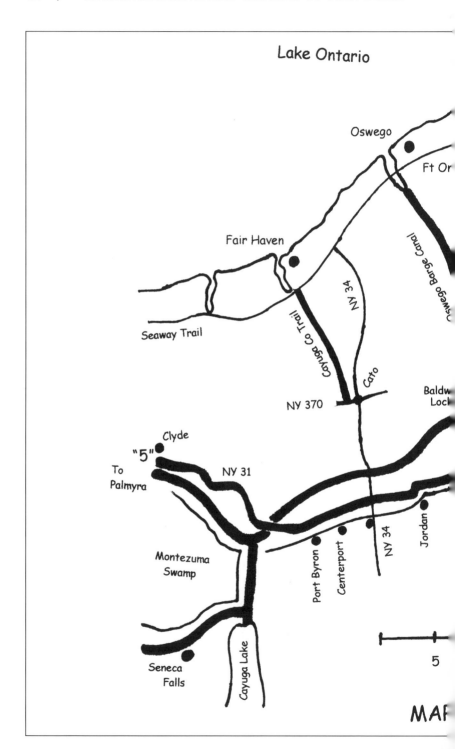

Lake Ontario

Oswego

Ft Or

Oswego Barge Canal

Fair Haven

NY 34

Cayuga Co Trail

Seaway Trail

Cato

NY 370

Baldw
Loc

Clyde

"5"

To
Palmyra

NY 31

NY 34

Jordan

Montezuma
Swamp

Port Byron

Centerport

Seneca
Falls

Cayuga Lake

5

MA

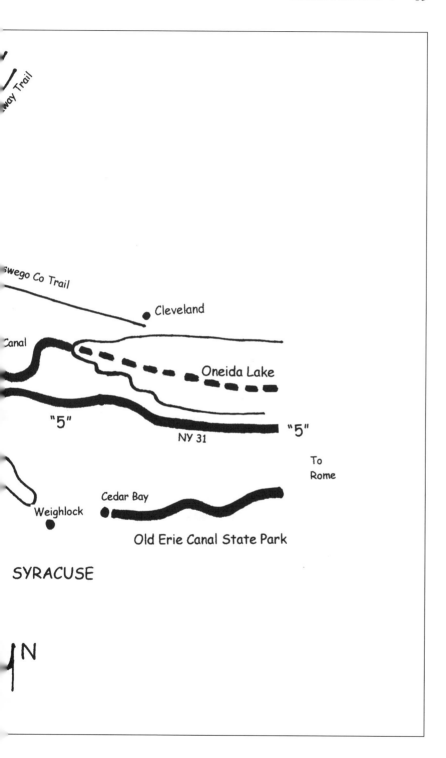

If you do some exploring on your own, anywhere between Syracuse and Rochester, you are likely to find, adjacent to the canal, an abandoned rail right of way. Don't confuse it with the canal towpath. The old railbed is all that remains of the New York West Shore & Buffalo Railroad. You can find more background on its history in the Mohawk Valley chapter. Just west of Port Byron is an old brick powerhouse. In the early part of this century, electric trolleys ran over the NYWS&B all the way from Buffalo to Ilion. In those days, a continuous network of trolleys, called "interurbans" extended from Upstate New York across the Midwest into central Wisconsin.

North of Weedsport, at Cato, a 15-mile railtrail extends north to Lake Ontario at Fair Haven. It is an eight mile ride on NY Route 34, another excellent state highway, from Weedsport to Cato. Cycling on Route 34 will bring you face to face with the extensive drumlin field that extends across the Lake Ontario plain. At one point, I've counted four drumlins, side-by-side. At Cato, turn left onto NY Route 370 and you will come to the unpaved railtrail in a very short distance. The railtrail extends north to Lake Ontario at Fair Haven, site of an excellent State Park. As Fair Haven is fifteen miles west of Oswego, a loop is quite practical. (See earlier insert on Oswego Canal.) The railtrail enters Fair Haven on Main Street, where you'll find a small sign "Cayuga County Trail" directing you "to Cato." It is just two-tenths of a mile to Fair Haven Beach State Park where you'll see unusual sculpted bluffs — the result of erosion of drumlins by Lake Ontario's wave action. Like other county-maintained trails, this railtrail is not always in the best condition. This railtrail sits on top of an old Lehigh Valley railbed. The Lehigh Valley used this line to reach its coal docks on Lake Ontario to export coal to Canada.

Erosion by ice is just one of the powerful forces of glaciation. The other is deposition, which is the movement and transfer of soils and rocks. A drumlin is a very visible result of deposition and there are about 10,000 "drumlins" in the Onondaga-Cayuga-Seneca area. This, too, is geologically extraordinary. Drumlins are small egg-shaped hills oriented in a north to south direction. They are typically about 200 feet tall and can be anywhere from 400 feet to a mile in length. The north face of the hill is always the steep slope. Drumlins are composed of fine soils deposited by running streams at the edge of a glacier. You'll see many. Indeed, a cycling itinerary "Death by Drumlins" extends north and west of Newark, in Wayne County. You can obtain the route description by contacting GFLRPC through the Resource Guide. When you see all these drumlins, or maybe cycle up and over, think of how cold it must have been here, just 10,000 years ago. The Earth was beginning a gradual warm up from the peak of the last "Ice Age," about 20,000 years ago, when many believe it was the coldest ever. If that warming is continuing today, it is just a part of that long trend.

Before you leave Cayuga County and enter Seneca County, you also have the option of visiting the nearby Montezuma National Wildlife Refuge. This is an enormous swamp — another glacial feature. Think of it an enormous plugged-up Finger Lake filled with muck. Creating a "waterproof" Erie Canal (that is, a canal bed that would hold canal water and not let it all seep out into the swamps) across this topography was another engineering challenge for canal builders. These same swamplands are a major bird sanctuary as well.

The Visitors Center is located south of Bike "5," (NY Route 31) on Route5 & 20. A slight detour will take you there. Look for the left turn on NY 89 and take it southbound. Right after you cross the Barge Canal (you can visit Lock 26), you'll see Tschache Pool up ahead. The flooded timber area of Tschache Pool is a heron rookery. Take a moment and look over the pool. Note the nests in the stark, dead trees in the distance. Some of these are bald eagle sites. In 1976, the Montezuma Refuge and NYS Department of Environmental Conservation began to release eagles at Montezuma. Through 1980, 23 eagles were released. Bald eagles have returned to Montezuma and have reared young. You can continue south on NY 89 and visit other unique sites in the 6432-acre Wildlife Refuge. The US Fish & Wildlife Service administers the Refuge. There is an information center located on Route 5 and 20 which is staffed in the summer and which has restrooms and an observation platform. The Service does not permit bikes on Refuge roads and trails; do not ride there without permission.

New York State Canal Corporation

Stopping at the Montezuma National Wildlife Refuge.

A Diversion — The Cayuga-Seneca Canal

The Cayuga-Seneca Canal extends twelve miles westward from Montezuma to Geneva. There are no special signs for this route, but it is worth exploring if you are interested in women's suffrage. This small region is rich in the history of women's rights and includes the Elizabeth Cady Stanton home, the National Women's Hall of Fame, and the Women's Rights National Historical Park. All are in the Village of Seneca Falls. Stopping here might give insights into how the prosperity brought by the opening of the Erie Canal, as well as the shortage of men during the Civil War, was linked to the emancipation of women in America. 1998 was the 150th Anniversary of the first Woman's Rights Convention, held in Seneca Falls in 1848, just thirteen years after completion of the canal.

The Cayuga-Seneca Canal will also take you to New York's two largest Finger Lakes. Most people consider five lakes to be "The Finger Lakes;" in reality there are many more. It may be that New York's Finger Lakes are its most distinctive and visible reminder of its glacial past. These lakes are unique geologic formations, somewhat similar to glacial lakes found in the European Alps. All have depths of several hundred feet. Seneca Lake is New York's deepest, extending to 618 feet; this is 174 feet below sea level. Cayuga Lake is 427 feet deep, which is 36 feet below sea level. These deeply scoured bottoms result from the tremendous erosion forces of ice and the enormous boulders carried along within the glacier.

New York's Finger Lakes have excellent state parks for camping and swimming and rest stops. It is beyond the scope of this guide to recommend cycling routes through the wine country of the Finger Lakes. Suffice it to say that most roads are in excellent shape for cycling and the countryside is beautiful and unique. If you should make it to the southern ends of Seneca or Cayuga Lake, you should be aware that these points, too, are on today's Barge Canal System. Because the Cayuga-Seneca Canal links the northern ends of these Lakes to the Erie Canal, places like Ithaca and Montour Falls have canal facilities and can be reached from the Atlantic Ocean or the Great Lakes by boat.

After visiting Seneca Falls, it is a 15-mile ride north, back to Clyde, to pick up the Erie Canal once again. You can go on to Geneva, the end of the Cayuga-Seneca Canal and head north to rejoin the Erie Canal at Lyons.

You will cross the New York portion of Bikecentennial's Northern Transcontinental Route in western Cayuga or eastern Wayne County. Their recommended route passes through Seneca Falls on the Cayuga-Seneca Canal and crosses Bike "5" near Savannah in Wayne County. The Bikecentennial route crosses New York's border with Pennsylvania west of Jamestown and crosses into Vermont via the ferry at Fort Ticonderoga, on Lake Champlain. (See Resource Section for more information.)

As there are so many canal options in this area, you might consider establishing a base in one of Cayuga County's attractive small canal towns. Based there, you can bike east as far as you like toward Syracuse one day, west to Seneca Falls the next, north to Lake Ontario the third, and on into Wayne County the next. A trip south to the vineyards of the Finger Lakes is possible too. You will find local roads in this area to be excellent for cycling, so both on and off-road tours are feasible.

To continue to follow the Erie Canal westward toward Buffalo, you'll need to be on Bike "5." Follow it across the Seneca River into Seneca County. It's a short ride across a portion of the Montezuma Swamp and, in less than one mile, you'll arrive at the border of Wayne County. Reset your odometer to zero once again.

The Erie Canal in Western New York

Lockport and the County of Niagara contain the greatest natural and artificial wonders [Niagara Falls and the Erie Canal, respectively], *second only to the wonders of freedom and equal rights.*
Marquis de Lafayette — 1825
(while at the Lockport construction site of the Erie Canal)

4 / *The Erie Canal in Western New York*

Cycling Western New York crosses territory that was essentially outside, or beyond, the frontiers of both the Dutch colony of Nieuw Amsterdam and the British colony of New York. The French considered this region part of "New France." After all, they had discovered and settled the Saint Lawrence and Mississippi River basins, and the waterways of this part of upstate New York flowed north into the Saint Lawrence, "their" river. After the French and Indian Wars, the British government had prohibited settlement "...beyond the Allegheny mountains." However, in this part of New York, thanks to the glacial epochs you have seen evidence of throughout your canal tour, there was no obvious Allegheny barrier, and the soils were especially fertile — so settlement did continue.

By now you know that there were four distinct "Erie Canals" in New York. However, in Western New York these generally overlap. As a result, for the most part, today's Barge Canal is on the original alignment of DeWitt Clinton's four foot deep "Ditch." This is for canal lovers. From here westward, the old Erie is still "alive" as a functioning canal. For the vast majority of the way, the original Erie Canal towpath is open for recreational use. Mostly, it is unpaved, but maintained in very good condition. There are many boat tours which you can combine with cycling. If you take a boat trip, it will be on the original route of the canal. Perhaps the greatest wonder is how the canal, still, is a vibrant, living part of the many small towns and villages through which it flows. You'll enjoy the many "canaltowns" along the way — they really know how to "celebrate" their canal.

Wayne County

Bike "5" and the Erie Canal run side-by-side across most of Wayne County. Bike "5" stays atop NY Route 31, an excellent roadway for cycling, and fulfills its role as your guide to the Erie Canal. It is easy to follow, in excellent condition, traffic volumes are low, and there are wide shoulders throughout. Bike "5" passes directly through charming farm villages like Savannah (MP 3), Clyde (MP 9), Lyons (MP 17), Newark (MP 23), Port Gibson, which is in Ontario County (MP 27), Palmyra (MP 30), and Macedon (MP 33). At MP 37 you'll come to the border with Monroe County. The area between Rochester and Syracuse, in Wayne, Seneca, and Cayuga, has some of the best roadways in New York State for cycling. Find a small town to stay and don't hesitate to explore.

There are many hidden Erie Canal treasures along the way. At MP 13, between Clyde and Lyons, look for a small sign "Canal Park." It is visible in both directions. This will take you to Wayne County's "Black Brook Area Canal Park" where there is good interpretive material on canal history and some stretches of well-maintained, unpaved, towpath to cycle. Less than a mile farther west on Bike "5" is Wayne County's "Lock Berlin Area Canal Park." It, too, has a well-maintained, grassy towpath for cycling. If you are riding high-pressure tires, you'll need to stay on Bike "5," but be sure to stop and see the old canal structures. If you are comfortable cycling on a hard grassy surface, you'll be able to tour some of this hidden towpath. As I stated in describing Cayuga County, there is a lot of old Erie Canal still waiting to be explored. Feel free to do so.

Louis Rossi

Wayne County Park at Lock Berlin has excellent interpretive data.

There is a lot of Barge Canal to see too. There is a pretty canalside park in Lyons at Barge Canal Lock 27. Lock 28, one mile west of Lyons, is right alongside Bike "5." This is the western maintenance hub for the Erie Canal and you might see barges or tugs in dry-dock. An old Erie Canal Lock lies just a bit west alongside Drydock Road. You will pass Lock 28B at Newark. Lock 29 in Macedon has interesting old Erie Canal structures right alongside.

As you ride across Wayne County, you'll see that the Erie Canal and New York Central are virtually adjacent. By 1851, ten little railroads stretched across the state. They were built adjacent to the canal for simple reasons. First, it was desirable to remove passenger traffic from the canals as a means of providing space for the growing canal freight trade. Secondly, the canal closed in winter. There was less disruption of commerce with the railroad in the same towns. Of course, the route was pretty "flat" making a railroad highly practical. In 1851, Erastus Corning created the "New York Central" from these small railroads; it was America's first truly large corporation. (The "Corning Trail" back in Albany is named for his grandson, Erastus Corning II, a longtime mayor of Albany.)

Palmyra (MP 30), the "birthplace" of Mormon, is of special interest. According to Mormon tradition, it was here, in AD 421, that Moroni, last survivor of an ancient people, buried the Mormon record. The record was revealed by the Angel Moroni to Joseph Smith in 1820. The Joseph Smith home and many other important Mormon sites make worthwhile visits. A Hill Cumorah Pageant takes place every July. Hill Cumorah is an ice-age drumlin. Palmyra has special "Canal Town Days" in September.

Don't miss the Canalway Trail which resumes in Palmyra at Lock 28B. This is the start of the longest continuous stretch of the trail and extends almost all the way to Lake Erie. Most of it is unpaved but kept in excellent condition. The riding surface of the unpaved towpath is hard enough to support almost any bicycle type including high-pressure tires.

Louis Rossi

At Palmyra, the Canalway Trail resumes and runs all the way to Lake Erie.

Immediately after it begins, the Canalway Trail goes over the Palmyra Aqueduct. You can get a great photo of it from Bike "5."

Cycling across this portion of New York, you'll pass through some of the state's most fertile farmlands. In addition to dairying, you'll see extensive fruit crops. Not surprisingly, these fruit crops flourish due to glacial processes. The Great Lakes and the Finger Lakes, all glacial remnants, support a slightly warmer and dependable microclimate that is ideal for fruit. A fall trip, during the apple harvest season, can be spectacular. I've cycled this region with friends from the state of Washington, a state well known for its apple crop. They have marveled at the variety of apples grown in New York state — at least 23 varieties are available at one time or another during the growing season. The enormous Kraft Foods plant you'll ride by in Macedon indicates the use for much of New York's dairy production — the manufacture of cheese products. (The New York State Department of Agriculture and Markets offers a "Guide to Farm Fresh Food" which may help direct you to fresh harvests.)

Monroe County

Reset your odometer. Bike "5" continues westward along Route 31. However, be aware that it follows busy streets and is not suitable for all cyclists. I don't recommend following it. Should you wish to ride on-road in Monroe County, I suggest you get the "Greater Rochester Area Bike Map," which is available through the Resource Guide. If you enter Monroe County on Bike "5," turn off at MP 3 and go to the Canalway Trail in the charming village of Fairport.

Fortunately, the Canalway Trail is 100 % complete across Monroe County. A mixture of paved and unpaved segments, it is the route you should follow. If you enter the county on the Canalway Trail that began in Palmyra, you'll come directly to the village of Fairport.

Fairport and the neighboring village, Pittsford, are leaders in their efforts to make their canal facilities attractive. Don't miss cycling through this segment of Erie Canal history. Along the way, the Canal rises 70 feet above the surrounding countryside. This is the "Great Embankment" and extends for about one mile. Choosing this route was one of the great engineering achievements of James Geddes, who was not an engineer. Geddes is responsible for discovering that the Genesee River, which would have to be used to supply water to the canal, was in fact high enough to fill a level embankment that hugged the ridge of the Irondequoit Valley. His achievement was this great level embankment that made an inland canal route feasible. Geddes later wrote:

While traversing these snowy hills in December, 1808, I little thought of ever seeing the Genesee waters crossing this valley on the embankment now constructing over it. I had, to be sure, lively presentiments, that time would bring about all I was planning, that boats would one day pass along on the tops of these fantastic ridges, that posterity would see and enjoy the sublime spectacle, but that for myself, I had been born many, very many years too soon. (Quoted from: Stars on the Water, Condon)

New York State Canal Corporation

The Great Embankment between Fairport and Pittsford is an engineering triumph

New York State Canal Corporation

Cycling along the canal east of Rochester.

Just west of Pittsford, today's Barge Canal diverges from the alignment of the original Erie Canal, which extended through downtown Rochester; the alignments rejoin west of the city. Also, just west of Pittsford, a short stretch of unimproved, unpaved bikepath

extends along the old canalbed to a park at old Erie Lock 62. The
Erie Canalway Trail follows the Barge Canal, past Barge Canal Lock
32 (also the site of a small park) and does not enter downtown Rochester. Lock 33 is the last lock on the Barge Canal until Lockport. It
begins another "Long Level" and is the longest flat stretch on the
present Erie Barge Canal. At Locks 32 or 33, you may see a busy and
active rail line. This is one of the few pieces of the old NYWS&B
(New York, West Shore & Buffalo) that is active today. It forms an
important mainline freight bypass of downtown Rochester.

Remember, you should be following the Erie Canalway Trail alongside the Barge Canal — don't follow Bike "5" through Rochester.

Before you head farther west, you may want to head south of
Fairport to the State Historic Site at Ganondogan. It is about seven
miles off-course, on a hilltop, south of the village of Victor. You
might want to look it up if you have become "hooked" on the history of the Iroquois Confederacy. Ganondogan (Gannagaro) was the
capital of the Seneca Nation; this was the "Western Door" to the
Iroquois Confederacy. The Senecas were the most powerful of the
Five Nations and, in fact, outnumbered the other four. Archeologists
have identified nearly thirty Seneca sites nearby. Grassy self-guided
trails wind through the Ganondogan State Historic Site. Why not
tie up the bikes and walk the trails?

The powerful Huron and Iroquois Indian nations, who lived in
these vast lands, had been at war long before the arrival of the French
in Canada and the British (and Dutch) in America. Foolishly, Samuel
de Champlain allowed himself to be drawn into these conflicts.
Goaded by their Huron Indian allies, the French had been battling
with the Iroquois since the day the first Frenchman, de Champlain,
set foot in New York. In 1609, just months before Henry Hudson
arrived on the Upper Hudson, de Champlain had fought a successful
battle against the Iroquois near present day Ticonderoga. Ironically,
his victory was a strategic defeat for the French.

In 1687, the French, under de Denonville destroyed the village of
Ganondogan. Since he could not vanquish the Seneca, de Denonville

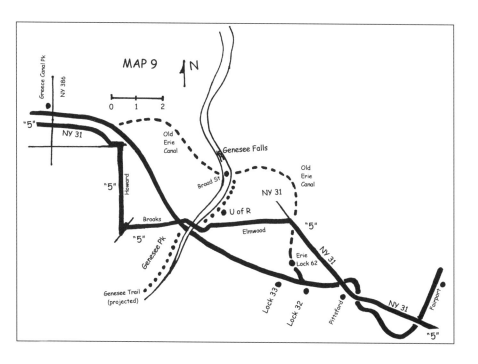

devastated their lands. His reports state that he burned storehouses with about 500,000 bushels of corn. The Seneca later attacked Montreal in retaliation and the Iroquois allied themselves with the British. Indeed, the Iroquois nation's defeat would ultimately come from the successful American forces which punished them for support of the British in the Revolution. Most had stayed loyal to the British to the end. In an embarrassment to many loyal British citizens, the Treaty of Paris which settled the Revolutionary War made no provision for their defeated Iroquois allies. Many relocated in Canada, after punitive raids by American forces destroyed their villages and crops. Subsequently, Jay's treaty of 1794 provided some relief to the Iroquois. (See Niagara County section for more.)

From Rochester, the 90-mile "Genesee Valley Greenway," now under construction, will extend southward in the near future. This will follow the Genesee Canal which once extended to Olean, near the Pennsylvania border. Indeed, for a short time there was a connection into Pennsylvania that could take you to Pittsburgh and Harrisburg. The Genesee Canal climbed over 1000 feet of elevation and required 112 locks to do so. The canal was abandoned in 1878. Much of it was reused as a rail line. Once reopened for cycling, this will be an excellent side trip as the old Genesee Canal passed through Letchworth Gorge, known as "the Grand Canyon of New York." To climb the falls here, 50 locks were required in just five miles. Letchworth is an excellent park for off-road mountain biking.

The Greenway will connect to the Canalway Trail in Genesee Valley Park which is just west of the Genesee River. A web site is available; see the Resource Guide.

A Special Note on Visiting Rochester

Rochester is the home of corporate giants like Kodak, Bausch & Lomb, and Xerox. Monroe County leads New York in international trade. Indeed, Monroe County alone exports more goods than most states. That is what the Empire State was once all about. The original Erie Canal did go through the heart of Rochester, just like Syracuse. There is nothing left to see. However, you can spot ruins of the Genesee Aqueduct, which carried the Erie Canal over the Genesee River. This was the second largest aqueduct on the canal system (800 feet long with 10 stone arches) and the only one totally intact. Today, that aqueduct carries Broad Street, a major commercial thorough-fare, across the Genesee River. From above, it is impossible to tell that you are cycling over an original Erie aqueduct. However from an adjacent bridge you'll be very impressed to see the old aqueduct "beneath" today's Broad Street.

You can get downtown by traveling through the University of Rochester and along local streets following the Genesee River. Today, the Genesee River is still a principal water supply for the Barge Canal. Rochester is famous for its Lilac Festival, held in May. The Lilac Festival has been held for ninety years.

There is an excellent, free resource, a "Greater Rochester Area Bike Map," which you should consult if you are planning an on-road bike trip in Monroe County. See the Resource Guide.

Louis Rossi

The original Erie Canal Aqueduct across the Genesee River still carries Broad Street in downtown Rochester.

Continuing west along the Canalway Trail, the Greece Town Park makes a good rest stop. Travel west through Spencerport, Adams Basin and Brockport. Spencerport celebrates Fireman's Days in June and Canal Days in July. The Fireman's Day parade drew 10,000 spectators to this small village in 1997 — it is one of the largest fireman's parades in Upstate New York. Notice the bridge carrying Main Street over the Canal. This, and fifteen more just like it in western New York, are unique "lift bridges." When a boat passes, the bridge "lifts" to permit the boat to pass beneath. What makes them unusual is the pedestrian walkways. When these were built, special accommodations were made so that pedestrians (and bicyclists) would not be disrupted. In its raised position, the bridge deck realigns itself with stairways and becomes an elevated walkway. The New York Department of Transportation has restored this and many other bridges like it. They deserve a special compliment for their careful treatment and respect for these historic structures.

Just west of Spencerport is the small hamlet of Adams Basin. Adjacent to another of the sixteen wonderful lift bridges over the Erie Canal is the Canalside Inn. If you saw Putnam's Store at Yankee Lock in Montgomery County or Sims Store in Onondaga County, you saw a "museum" of an old-time canal store. The Canalside Inn, a Bed & Breakfast today, is a living canal building, and the most interesting of the three. The oldest parts of the inn date from the construction of the Erie Canal. The interiors are perfectly preserved.

New York State Canal Corporation

Greece Canal Park. Many canal municipalities have police patrols on bikes.

Brockport is the home on a major campus of the State University of New York and the largest village in this part of Monroe county.

If you wish to cycle on-road, you can pick up Bike "5," in Brockport and follow it west. But there are many quieter local roads closer, or adjacent to the canal which you may find more attractive for cycling.

Whether on or off-road, soon you will come to the border of Monroe and Orleans Counties. It is 40 miles across Monroe County on the Canalway Trail.

Orleans County

Imagine finding a totally level line across a county. Now, imagine finding a level line across almost three counties. That's what Barge Canal engineers found and that is why there are no locks in Orleans County. The closest lock to the east is Lock 33 near Pittsford and the closest lock to the west is in Lockport. This "Long Level," extending for over 70 miles, makes for wonderful cycling. For the most part, you are following the "shoreline" of ancient Lake Iroquois, a major glacial lake. The flat "beach" made this engineering trick possible.

As you cycle westward through Orleans and Niagara Counties, you will never be far from the shore of Lake Ontario; typically, less than ten miles separates the lake from the canal. As there are many state parks along the Lake Ontario shoreline and the Seaway Trail identifies a good cycling route, feel free to experiment and add some attractive farm country, and maybe a swim, to your trip. Also running parallel to the canal, just a bit to the north, is NY Route 104. Local folk call this "Ridge Road." The ridge is, indeed, the shoreline of the ancient glacial lake.

That introduces us to another bit of unique Upstate history that derives from the last "Ice Age,"— cobblestone buildings. Cobblestones are small rounded stones created by thousands of years of wave action. The shores of ancient glacial Lake Iroquois were littered with these glacial features which at first were an annoyance to farmers.

However, the prosperity brought by the Canal enabled these stones to be used in construction of homes and churches. About 700 cobblestone landmarks extend across Upstate with most being located along the Lake Ontario shore. You will not cycle far along NY 104, for example, without passing one of these unique structures. Although cobblestone construction extended into the Midwest, probably eighty percent of all surviving structures are in upstate New York. Wayne, Monroe and Orleans Counties have at least 100 each.

Louis Rossi

The Canalway Trail and Bike "5" are close to each other in Orleans County.

Like Wayne and Monroe, Orleans County is real Erie Canal territory. It is also rich farmland, specializing in fruit crops. You'll need to cycle north or south of the canal to find the best farmlands. The Canalway Trail and Bike "5" are close to each other, enabling a cyclist to choose either route. There are many excellent local roads too, so feel free to explore. Not too far away is the Seaway Trail, which hugs the Lake Ontario Shore. In Orleans and Niagara Counties, the Seaway Trail offers some good on-road cycling options.

There are three "canaltowns" in Orleans County. First, you'll come to Holley, named for an early Canal Commissioner. Holley recently received a $1 million grant to develop recreational trails adjacent to the canal which will link to nearby sites. There is a "Depot Museum" in Holley which will explain some of the local rail history. The larger villages of Albion (MP 11), and Medina (MP 20) are especially inviting. Here, a tourist can experience the canal in a small village context. As the canal is on original alignment, and these well-kept villages are creations of the canal, something of the real Erie Canal "ambiance" is preserved here. You might want to visit the Cobblestone Museum in Albion or the Strawberry Festival in June. Medina celebrates the canal with a Canal Festival each July.

It was a level route across Orleans County for Erie Canal builders, so there are no locks to see. However at MP 17, just east of Medina at Culvert Road, there is something unique in all of New York. Here, the canal crosses over Culvert Road; both boats and bikes "sail" over the roadway traffic below; this is the only highway "tunnel" under the Canal. This unique tunnel was a feature of the original Erie Canal and was retained when the expanded Erie Barge Canal was built. Be sure to bike under the canal, too. (Yes, it drips!) Also near Medina, the canal passes over an aqueduct above a waterfall. The Orleans County Planning Department has mapped some cycling routes to historic points of interest; see the Resource Guide.

There is an unusually nice stretch of Bike "5" between Medina and Middleport, in Niagara County. Here, Bike "5" follows NY 31E and is directly adjacent to the canal.

The railroad you have been following is the Falls Road, first opened in 1837. Years ago, this formed an important New York Central System route from Rochester to Niagara Falls, across Canada to Detroit, and on to Chicago. Today, most of the Falls Road in New York and Canada is closed or serves only local traffic. There is a handsome brick and stone depot on Main Street in Medina.

It is 24 miles across Orleans County on Bike "5."

Louis Rossi

Culvert Road in Orleans County is the only roadway under the canal.

Niagara County

Niagara County, too, is a rich farmland. Farmers harvest nearly ten million grapes here each year. Apples, cherries, various berries, peaches, pears, plums and prunes make up the rest of the harvest. There is a Peach Festival in Lewiston in September and an Apple Festival in Lockport in October. Niagara County is one of the most cycle-friendly counties in New York State. There are many excellent local roads, pretty villages, important history, and world famous scenery.

If you entered Niagara County on Bike "5" you will be on NY 31E, which ends in Middleport. This is a short stretch of state high-way that is directly adjacent to the Canal. If you are following the Erie Canalway Trail on top of the canal bed, you will arrive in Middleport as well. There you'll find a very large 1841 cobblestone landmark, the First Universalist Church, on South Main Street. The church's cobblestones were gathered at congregational picnics orga-nized for this purpose. Niagara County has published a guide to fifty cobblestone landmarks located throughout the county.

After Middleport and Gasport, you will come to Lockport (MP 12), which is another "must see" for canal buffs. (These three "ports" tell us by their names that they were founded after the canal was built.) At Lockport, the final 50-foot climb to the 565-foot elevation level of Lake Erie takes place. The original five locks of the Erie Canal and today's double lock of the Barge Canal stand side-by-side. This is another unique sight. Here, the difference between early 19th century engineering and early 20th century engineering stand starkly in contrast. On today's Barge Canal, Lock 35 is the final lock. The topmost lock on the old Erie Canal was Lock 71. (When first built, the original Erie Canal had 83 locks.) There is a small Erie Canal Museum at the site. There are boat tours through the flight of locks. This is the final climb is the Niagara Escarpment, which is about 160 feet high in all and takes us above the ancient shore of ancient glacial Lake Iroquois to the level of modern Lake Erie. Once on top, it is a flat ride to Buffalo or Niagara Falls. There are no more locks.

At Lockport, the long stretch of Canalway Trail which extends across Western New York ends. The Canal turns southwest and enters Erie County in the Town of Amherst. Bike "5" continues directly west, along Route 31, to Niagara Falls. This presents a tough choice. A good option is to make Lockport your base, cycle east one day and return to Lockport. The next day, make a loop to Niagara Falls and back. Finally, on a third day, a round-trip to Buffalo is practical. See the map on the next page.

Niagara Falls remains one of the great natural wonders of the world, less than 20 miles due west of Lockport. Bike "5" will take you to the Rainbow Bridge almost adjacent to the Falls. A cyclist should visit the New York State Reservation on Goat Island. The many quiet vantage points on Goat Island offer the best perspectives of the Falls and a bicycle is the best way to get around to all of them. There is so much to see along the Niagara River, in two countries, that you should visit a Tourist Information Center. Plan to set aside at least a full day, perhaps two, for bicycle touring.

Niagara Falls is about 20
miles from Lockport.

Niagara County

While cycling in the area, you might notice the Tuscarora Indian Reservation. Who are the Tuscaroras? These peoples are the sixth tribe to join the "Five Nations" and that is why many people refer to the Iroquois as "the Six Nations." The Tuscaroras were full members of the League, but only arrived in New York in the early 1700s. By then, the Iroquois League was already very old.

If you visit the Falls, you may want to complete your tour of important battlefield sites with a visit to Fort Niagara, twelve miles north, where the Niagara River enters Lake Ontario. Begun by the French at the time of La Salle, in 1679, the present fort dates from 1726. Fort Niagara was an important base of operations against American revolutionaries. It was used to arm and supply the Seneca and other Iroquois tribes who were fighting for the British. After the Revolution, and after destruction of their homes and farms by the Americans, many Iroquois relocated to the Niagara Frontier and settled on both sides of the river. Jay's Treaty of 1794 gave the Iroquois the free right to "pass and repass" across the national border. Indian tribes in New York, Ontario, and Quebec have this right to this day. Every year, in July an Indian "Border Crossing Celebration" takes place near Niagara Falls. There is an Indian parade across the border, unchecked by immigration officers, and many other celebrations of Indian rights and customs.

Fort Niagara played a major role in unsuccessful American invasions of Canada in the War of 1812. It was captured by the British late in 1813, and may very well be the last piece of continental America to have been captured in warfare and occupied by a foreign power.

In retaliation for the American burning of the village of Niagara, most of the American settlements along the Niagara were put to the torch by the British. Just a year before, Thomas Jefferson had written: *"The acquisition of Canada this year, as far as the neighborhood of Quebec, will be a mere matter of marching, and will give us experience for the attack on Halifax the next, and the final expulsion of England from the continent."* (Quoted from: <u>Stars on the Water</u>, Condon)

NYS Office of Parks and Recreation/Niagara Region

Fort Niagara is a great stone bastion begun by the French in 1679.

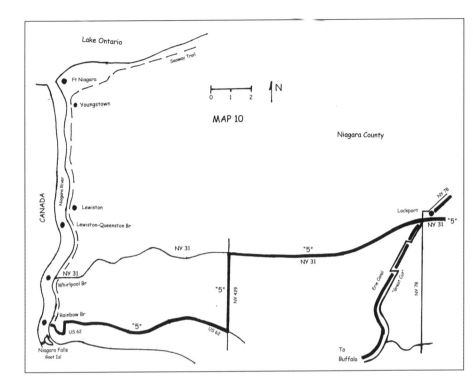

Instead of annexing Canada, the American invasions did much to encourage the small Canadian provinces to unify. Luckily, the fledgling American republic did not lose the War of 1812 to England, and peace was finally achieved on the border.

A Special Note on Visiting Canada

Cross over one of the Niagara Falls bridges to Canada. Each of the three bridges between the United States and Canada is bicycle-friendly and offers different perspectives on the Falls, the whirlpools, and river below. In Queenston, Canada, you can get the Canadian version of the War of 1812.

The Niagara Peninsula of Ontario is a wonderful place for cycling. Unfortunately, year-by-year, crossing the border between the United States and Canada gets more difficult. If you intend to cross the border, be sure to bring along a photo ID. Technically, a driver's license is not sufficient — bring a passport or copy of your birth certificate. All of this ever-tightening border control is most unfortunate and totally inconsistent with the history of the region.

Less than twenty miles from the Niagara River lies the "granddaddy" of canals in this region — the Welland Canal. This is not a "barge" canal designed for small craft, but a full-fledged "ship" canal, part of the Saint Lawrence Seaway system. Much of the Welland Canal is accessible to cyclists.

Let's get back to the central purpose of our tour, the Erie Canal, which went southwest from Lockport to Buffalo. Just west of Lockport, the canal enters the "Great Cut." This rock cut extends for more than six miles and is about 30 feet deep. It is impressive today; imagine excavating it almost two hundred years ago. The boat excursions through the locks at Lockport also extend into the "Great Cut." This is the best way to experience it.

Louis Rossi

The flight of locks at Lockport, old and new, stand side-by-side.
Their construction was a wonder to the Marquis de Lafayette.

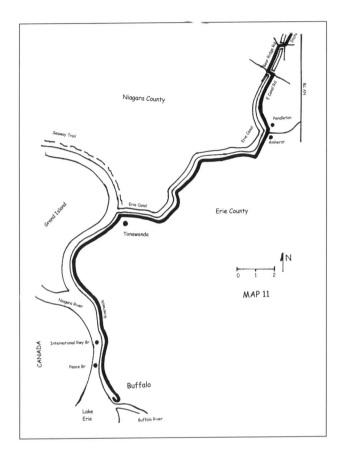

Niagara County

Seaway Trail

Grand Island

Erie Canal

Tonawanda

Niagara River

Riverwalk

CANADA

International Rwy Br

Peace Br

Buffalo

Lake
Erie

Buffalo River

Erie Canal

Pendleton

Amherst

Erie County

Bear Ridge Rd

E Canal Rd

State

NY 78

N

0   1   2

MAP 11

To follow the Erie Canal to Buffalo, leave Bike "5" in Lockport. As this book goes to press, the old towpath through the Great Cut is being cleared and its opening for recreational use should come soon. Right now, you'll need to follow local streets to Pendleton. There are no markings along this route. As there are no route markers to guide you, you are somewhat on your own, but following the canal is not difficult. First, find "State Road" along the south embankment of the canal, just off Bike "5" at Transit Street. Take State Road to Summit Street. Make a jog across the Canal and turn again to follow the canal's other embankment along Bear Ridge Road. When you come to Lockport Road (Robinson Road), cross back again over the Canal to East Canal Road. Follow East Canal Road. You will arrive in Pendleton, which lies on the border of Niagara County. All the time, the Canal will be adjacent to you. Cross the Tonawanda Creek and enter Erie County. It is only six miles from Lockport to the Erie County border. This is not as difficult as it sounds.

In total, it is 32 miles across Niagara County if you head for Niagara Falls and 18 miles if you head for Pendleton.

Erie County

Enter Amherst. Once you are in Erie County, the riding is a pleasant canalside trip. Here, both the original Erie Canal and the Barge Canal use Tonawanda Creek. Take the very first right onto Tonawanda Creek Road. You'll cycle past the Amherst Town Museum, along quiet roads, past marinas and small parks between Amherst and Tonawanda. Follow Tonawanda Creek Road, Creek Drive, and East Niagara Street alongside the Canal. Again, there are no route markers to guide you, but by keeping the canal on your right, westbound, you will easily find your way. (A "Bicycle Route Guide: Buffalo/ Niagara Falls Area" is available from The Greater Buffalo Convention and Visitors Bureau. See the Resource Section.) There are some bikepaths along the canal in this area too. These are not built on top of any canal facilities but feel free to take them; you won't get lost. It is ten miles to the mouth of the Tonawanda Creek (the Barge Canal) at the Niagara River.

As you enter Tonawanda, you'll come to the historic Long Homestead (1829). At Main Street in Tonawanda, the Erie Canalway Trail resumes (here it is called "Riverwalk") and extends to Buffalo along the Niagara River. The Niagara River isn't really a river; it is a "strait" connecting two Great Lakes. You'll be amazed at how rapidly this river flows. The "Riverwalk" is not fully complete, but the incomplete on-road segments are clearly marked and easy to follow.

Follow "Riverwalk." You'll go right by the federal lock which guards the western entrance to the Barge Canal. All this lock really does is adjust for wind-driven changes in the level of Lake Erie. You won't be able to see the old Erie Canal; it is buried beneath the adjacent interstate highway.

Here, where the Canal joins the waters of Lake Erie, stop for a moment, and reflect on the achievement that the Erie Canal represents. In a wilderness, a small and not-so-prosperous state, emerging from more than a century of violent warfare, undertook on its own, with no help from the Federal Government, to build a vast waterway, largely in stone. New York had sought help from the Federal Government; President Jefferson was said to have remarked:
"It is a splendid project and may be executed in a century hence....but it is little short of madness to think of it in this day."

In this century, the state, now truly the Empire State (due in no small part to the Erie Canal), took it upon itself to enlarge that waterway at the same time that the Federal Government was constructing the Panama Canal. The Erie is ten times longer than the Panama and has many more structures, some of which are the largest of their kind ever built. While no longer important in the movement of goods, the Erie is re-emerging as a unique and historic recreational resource, unparalleled in America. Maybe its heyday is yet to come.

As you come to downtown Buffalo, you'll cycle beneath the giant International Railway Bridge and the Peace Bridge. The International Railway Bridge celebrated its 125th birthday in 1998. Following "Riverwalk," you'll come onto Squaw Island. At its southern tip is a truly unique ride opportunity. The breakwater (or "mole") that shelters the riverfront from the fierce currents of the Niagara is open for cyclists, walkers, and fishermen. Ride out on it. It extends about a mile and a half. You'll have the mighty Niagara on one side, and the canal on the other. To me, it was like cycling at sea. You'll go beneath the giant Peace Bridge which deserves special mention as its name is no accident. The Peace Bridge commemorates the century of peace which the New York and Ontario border had shared at the time the bridge was opened early in this century. Almost another century of peace has gone by since then. In the history of the world, this is no little thing.

Finally, as you reach the waterfront in downtown Buffalo, ride out into Waterfront Park. It was 24 miles from your start across Erie County in Amherst. Enjoy this pleasant park. This was the terminus of the Erie Canal in the 19th century. You made it! You might just spot a lake steamer entering the Buffalo River with a load of grain for one of the few still-operating mills. A hundred years ago, this was cargo ultimately destined for the Eastern Seaboard via the Erie Canal; today it is most likely to go by rail. If it is cargo ultimately destined for Europe, it will not stop in Buffalo at all, but traverse the Welland Canal and the Saint Lawrence Seaway.

A Special Note on Visiting Buffalo.

Buffalo is one of my favorite cities. It is a beautiful city with a network of parks laid out by Frederic Law Olmstead. The Lake Erie waterfront is clean and attractive. Buffalo contains great architecture: four homes by Frank Lloyd Wright, Louis Sullivan's first "skyscraper," a music hall by Eero Saarinen, and many other gems. It has, in my opinion, Upstate New York's best food — from local favorites like "Beef on Weck" and "Wings," to international cuisines. The Albright-Knox Gallery is a great museum of art in a beautiful park setting. Buffalo enjoys these things today because it was the terminal of the Erie Canal. The canal "made" Buffalo one of the most important commercial centers of America in the 19th century. If you have the time, Buffalo is worth a visit.

If you are at Waterfront Park, all of downtown is nearby. Buffalo City Hall has an outdoor observation deck on its 28th floor. On a clear day, go and enjoy its commanding panorama and look back on your tour. Buffalo City Hall itself is an architectural gem; it is the largest city hall in America. You can safely cycle Buffalo streets on weekends.

There is a complete off-road bike path network from Fort Erie, Canada, directly across the Peace Bridge from Buffalo, to Niagara-on-the-Lake, Canada, directly across from Fort Niagara.

If you have the time, the Bicycle Museum in nearby Orchard Park, New York, is well worth visiting. It contains over 300 rare bicycles and thousands of bicycle artifacts.

Finally, if you are intent on heading west, there is the Seaway Trail to follow to New York's border with Pennsylvania, about 60 miles west along Lake Erie's southern shore.

This ends our Albany to Buffalo Erie Canal tour. However, if you are riding this tour from west-to-east, this will be your starting point. For secure, long-term parking in Buffalo, I would suggest using one of the nearby hotel garages near Waterfront Park.

The Champlain Canal and Glens Falls Feeder Canal

The rude path, which originally formed their line of communication, had been widened for the passage of wagons; so that the distance that had been traveled by the son of the forest in two hours, might easily be effected by a detachment of troops, with the necessary baggage, between the rising and setting of a summer sun. The loyal servants of the British crown had given to one of these forest-fastnesses the name of William Henry, and to the other that of Fort Edward, calling each after a favorite prince of the royal family.

The Glens Falls Feeder Canal Heritage Trail and the Warren County Bikeway follow the route described in great detail in The Last of the Mohicans.

5 / *The Champlain Canal and Glens Falls Feeder Canal*

The Champlain Canal was built to connect the Hudson River, which flows south to the Atlantic, with Lake Champlain which flows north into the Saint Lawrence River. The history of the Champlain Canal is closely linked with that of the Erie Canal. Both were begun in 1817, soon after peace came to a territory that had known brutal warfare for over a century. Both followed unsuccessful attempts by private companies to construct navigational improvements. At just 60 miles in length, the Champlain Canal opened in 1823, two years earlier than the Erie. Somehow, the Champlain never seemed to "get respect." Perhaps that was because a canal linking the northern end of Lake Champlain and the Saint Lawrence River, all in Canada, was not completed until 1858. Perhaps it was because of America's fascination with the opening and settlement of the West. In any case, the Champlain, like the Erie, was a vast commercial success. Also like the Erie, and important to us here, is the role the route plays in linking together much of early American history.

The major highlights of the Champlain Canal Tour are at Waterford, Saratoga Battlefield, and Glens Falls/Lake George. These are about 50 miles apart. While one could cycle the entire route, out-and-back, in one very hard day, this would not be wise. An option to consider is basing yourself in Saratoga Springs. You can cycle to Waterford and tour the battlefield one day, then cycle to Glens Falls and Lake George the next. This will still be a fast-paced tour. There is so much to see that allowing three or even four days would be wise depending on your cycling abilities and interest in history.

You can obtain a guide to the great sites along the almost 400-mile Hudson/Champlain corridor, between New York City and the Canadian border near Montreal, from state agencies. (See Appendix III.) I will focus on the 60-mile Champlain Canal and the fascinating history of the region it serves.

Saratoga County

The original Champlain Canal diverged from the Erie Canal north of Albany and crossed into Saratoga County near Cohoes. Unlike the Erie Canal, which had to climb the Cohoes Falls to head west, the Champlain followed its own more-or-less water-level route from Albany through Cohoes to Whitehall. It crossed the Mohawk River into Saratoga County behind a protective dam located near the NY Rt. 32 bridge. As of this writing, a small portion of the old Champlain Canal is open to tourists. This short section stretches between Fulton Street and the Lock 2 Canal Park in Waterford. It is unpaved, but a stop that you should be sure to make.

Therefore, before you head north, go back to Chapter 1 and read about the Champlain Canal in the Capital Region. After you have visited all the important sites in Waterford, you are now ready to start north, on Bike "9." from Waterford. It is just about 60 miles to Lake Champlain at Whitehall and it's packed with history. A lot has happened in this short distance. Reset your odometer to MP 0.

Back in the early 1800s, the original Champlain Canal was built parallel to but entirely separate from the Hudson River. The original Champlain Canal followed the west shore of the Hudson northward from Waterford in Saratoga County and crossed to the east shore in

Washington County just north of Schuylerville. It followed the east shore northward to Fort Edward. Efforts are being made to open the old towpath for recreational use. It is largely intact, waiting to be redeveloped. You will see many signs of the old Champlain Canal alignment as you pedal north.

Bike "9" turns north onto 3rd Street in Waterford. In two miles you will pass a historic marker indicating the furthest north point reached by the crew of Henry Hudson. In the same year that Henry Hudson's crew reached this point, just a few months earlier in 1609, Samuel de Champlain reached what is now Ticonderoga. There, at the instigation of his Huron allies, de Champlain launched a punitive raid against the Iroquois. This began more than a century of hostility between the Iroquois and the French. Sadly too, on his way back down the Hudson River, Henry Hudson found himself at war with the local Indians.

Continue north, passing through Mechanicville to Stillwater (MP 11). There is a canal park at Lock 4 in Stillwater. From Stillwater, for the next dozen miles, you will be passing through the various historical sites that comprised the Saratoga Battlefield. It is an understatement to say that historic markers abound. There are plenty on both sides of the Hudson, identifying all the sites of the many skirmishes that took place as the British tried to attack and then retreat from the blocking American forces. At MP 16 is the entrance to the National Historical Park. Be sure to take this detour. There is an entrance fee for cyclists. The park contains a nine-mile loop road (paved) that will take you to all the important sites of the Battle of 1777. Allow yourself several hours as the National Park Service has done a wonderful job of highlighting the principal events of the multi-day battle which took place here. The loop is a quiet one-way roadway which takes you to the commanding "heights" which the American forces had occupied to halt the British advance. The interpretive center will give you much information about the many battles that comprised this campaign which extended into Hubbardton (near

Rutland, Vermont) and Walloomsac (near Bennington, Vermont). This was no small campaign. It included naval engagements on Lake Champlain. I, for one, never ceased to be impressed at how so many thousands of troops, of many nationalities, were assembled and competently commanded, in what was certainly a vast wilderness.

Louis Rossi

The Saratoga Battlefield Monument.

One of America's most competent commanders in this complex battle, and the founder of the American navy at Whitehall (which comes near the end of this tour), was Benedict Arnold. There is a memorial to him at the battlefield, but, as he had subsequently deserted and gone to the British side, and "Benedict Arnold" had become synonymous with "traitor," his name was omitted. You'll see this on the park loop road. At the 155-foot obelisk commemorating the Battle at Schuylerville, there are spaces for four enormous statues. The one blank wall is for Arnold.

Had General Burgoyne succeeded in reaching Albany, and the British campaign in the Mohawk Valley been successful, the Colonies would have been split in two. Instead, the defeat at Saratoga, coupled with the losses in the Mohawk Valley at Oriskany and Fort Stanwix were the first major American victories. The prospect of defeating the British brought the essential French support that was necessary for the Revolution to succeed.

When you exit the park, return to Bike "9" and continue north. At Schuylerville (MP 24), the Schuyler House (1777) where General Burgoyne surrendered is at your roadside. Hopefully, you visited the Schuyler Mansion in Albany; this was their summer home. Also near Schuylerville is the 155-foot tall Saratoga Battlefield Monument, a short distance off-route in Victory Mills. Road signs will help you locate it easily.

Follow Bike "9" north from Schuylerville. Just outside the village, look for the "Canal Park" at Barge Canal Lock 5. There is an old Champlain Canal Lock at this small park. Continuing north, cross the Hudson River (MP 26) into Washington County (MP 0).

Washington County

It is a pleasant and very scenic ten mile trip northward along the Hudson to Fort Edward. Along the way you will find many historic markers dealing with the Champlain Canal, the French and Indian War and the Revolutionary War.

About a mile into Washington County, you'll see a sign for the old Champlain Canal Lock 12 on your right. A mile further (MP 2), at the entrance to Champlain Barge Canal Lock 6, there's a stone marker identifying the route General Knox used to bring Fort Ticonderoga's cannon to George Washington at Boston. General Knox brought the cannon down frozen Lake George, then overland through Fort Edward and down along the Hudson to Troy. He then began eastward into Massachusetts. You can take the small road which passes across the canal. It will take you close to the Hudson River, past the site of Fort Miller (1693), and return you to Bike "9" further north.

Louis Rossi

The site of Jane McCrae's slaughter.

Along "9", you will pass the site of Jane McCrae's July 27, 1777 slaughter, at MP 7 (she was later interred in Fort Edward, near MP 11). The murder of Jane McCrea, by Indians in General Burgoyne's army, was an important milestone in the Revolutionary War. Daughter of a loyalist, she was being escorted to the British lines when she was killed. This action galvanized anti-British sentiment throughout the colonies, and brought thousands of militia into the war. If British-allied Indians were going to kill loyalist civilians, what would they do to revolutionary families? Remember, too, the massacre of the British troops and civilians evacuating Fort William Henry in the French and Indian wars was not too distant in time or place.

Barge Canal Locks 6 through 12 (there is no Lock 10) in Washington County are good rest stops, or base points for day trips. The old Champlain Canal required a total of only twenty locks between Albany and Whitehall. Keep a sharp lookout for old canal ruins.

Louis Rossi

The old Champlain Canal Aqueduct near Fort Edward.

You'll pass Barge Canal Lock 7 as you enter Ft. Edward (MP 10). You'll immediately encounter a number of historic sites. Excavations are underway at the site of the encampment of Roger's Rangers; this was the launching point for one of America's major invasions of Canada. Over 15,000 soldiers once camped at this site. Visit the Old Fort House (1772), which is immediately on your left as you enter town. The museum is really a complex of five buildings and contains an exhibit on Jane McCrea. Almost opposite the Museum, across Bike "9," is an old Champlain Canal aqueduct.

Louis Rossi

More canal aqueduct ruins at Fort Edward.

At Fort Edward, the Hudson River turns westward. Here, you have options. I'll describe the ride to Whitehall first. This follows both the original and today's Champlain Canal, continuing northward in Washington County over a slight raise in land elevation, through Fort Ann (MP 22) to Whitehall (MP 32). Whitehall is the birthplace of the American navy. There are interesting naval artifacts to see. If you find this hard to believe, remember, Lake Champlain is an international waterway which played a critical role in the battles for possession of North America between England and France.

Louis Rossi

The site of Fort Edward.

In Whitehall, in 1775, Benedict Arnold commissioned the first ship and the first fleet which would become the U.S. Navy. With a fleet of seventeen small ships, fourteen of which were built at Whitehall, Arnold sailed north to engage a British fleet near Plattsburgh in 1776. Although most of Arnold's fleet was ultimately captured or destroyed by the British in a three-day battle, its very existence had delayed invasion plans. This important engagement in the British campaign to descend the Champlain Valley to Albany was ultimately resolved at Saratoga. Here you can see historic naval artifacts, including the hull of the USS Niagara from the War of 1812.

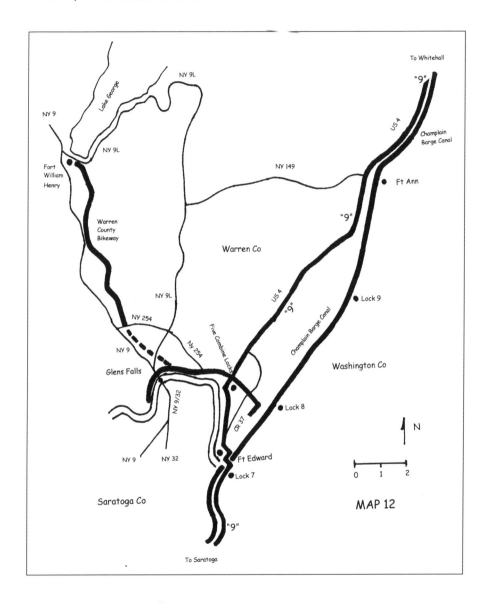

MAP 12

Going north to Whitehall is easy: Bike "9" follows NY Route 4 directly there. This is an excellent, fast cycling route through rolling hills and farms. You'll pass the "summit" section of the Champlain Barge Canal, which extends for six miles between Locks 8 and 9. The Glens Falls Feeder Canal helps keep this summit full of water.

Throughout this portion of your trip, the modern Champlain Canal sits on top of the original canal alignment. The Champlain Canal "summit" is about 120 feet above sea level. A rise of just 120 feet is all that separates the Atlantic waters from those that flow into the Saint Lawrence. That's the work of glaciers. As you speed by, think of General Burgoyne's troops. They moved southward in this area at barely one mile per day because a thousand American troops, under General Schuyler, moved ahead of them felling trees, flooding trails, and otherwise imposing obstacles to their forward progress.

You can stop at Lock 11, between Fort Ann and Whitehall, for a rest. When you reach Whitehall, continue on Bike "9" until you see a sign for "Lock 12 Marina." Turn here. It will take you to the center of town, alongside the canal and to the museum sites. Lock 12 marks the end of the Champlain Canal. Ahead lies Lake Champlain, named for Samuel de Champlain who discovered it almost 400 years ago.

Louis Rossi

Whitehall is at the north end of the Champlain Canal, the south end of Lake Champlain, and is the birthplace of the U.S. Navy.

As you look at Lake Champlain, remember that it, too, results from glacial processes. Lake Champlain's surface elevation is less than 100 feet above sea level. Like other glacial lakes in New York, its bottom has been scoured below sea level to depths of up to 400 feet. Its virtual sea-level passage between the Adirondacks and Green Mountains results from glaciation. Glacial epochs ("ice ages") are extremely rare. The most recent one was one of the greatest ever. The beautiful and unique scenery you see is its result.

The other alternative is to leave the Champlain Canal and Bike "9" and go by bike path westward into Warren County. You'll trace an important feeder canal beside the Hudson to Glens Falls and go north on a converted rail trail to Lake George. Along this route, you'll see the most important sites of the French and Indian Wars.

Louis Rossi

The Warren County Bikeway is an excellent
paved route from Glens Falls to Lake George.

Tough choice? Do both. I'll describe a practical loop option at the end of the Warren County text. In 1777, General Burgoyne used both routes simultaneously to move his Army southward. If you can only do one, I recommend going to Warren County.

Should you be planning to cycle further north toward Canada, read the following narrative on Warren County.

Warren County

The best preparation for cycling northwest to Lake George is to read The Last of the Mohicans by James Fenimore Cooper. Cooper accurately describes the history that took place here, and all the important sites he painstakingly described are here to see.

The opening chapter of The Last Of The Mohicans tells us:

It was a feature peculiar to the colonial wars of North America, that the toils and dangers of the wilderness were to be encountered before the adverse hosts could meet. A wide and apparently impervious boundary of forests severed the possessions of the hostile provinces of France and England. The hardy colonist, and the trained European who fought at his side, frequently expended months in struggling against the rapids of the streams, or in effecting the rugged passes of the mountains, in quest of an opportunity to exhibit their courage in more martial conflict. But, emulating the patience and self-denial of the practiced native warriors, they learned to overcome every difficulty; and it would seem that, in time, there was no recess of the woods so dark, nor any secret place so lovely, that it might claim exemption from the inroads of those who had pledged their blood to satiate their vengeance, or to uphold the cold and selfish policy of the distant monarchs of Europe.
Perhaps no district throughout the wide extent of the immediate frontiers can furnish a livelier picture of the cruelty and fierceness of the savage warfare of those periods than the country which lies between the headwaters of the Hudson and the adjacent lakes.

For those interested in the French and Indian Wars, there are many sights to see. Fort William Henry (1755) is faithfully recreated at Lake George (Lac du Saint Sacrament to the French). The Marquis de Montcalm, heading up a force of 10,000, attacked and defeated the British defenders of the fort. The fort was destroyed. Contrary to the terms of surrender, Montcalm's Indian allies massacred the British and colonials. There are a number of historic markers in close proximity to the fort which help interpret the complex warfare which took place here. The Warren County Bikeway retraces the route of the British retreat — as you cycle the scenic countryside, you will be cycling over the very site of the massacre. The bikeway will deposit you at the fort where you can see thousands of historic artifacts.

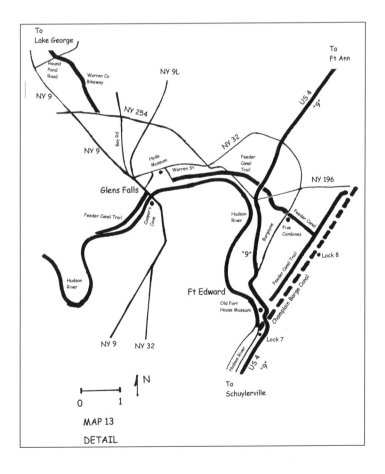

My recommended route diverts from Bike "9" in Fort Edward. You'll leave the route of the Champlain Canal and follow the Glens Falls Feeder Canal instead. Most of this route is off-road.

The route is as follows: At Fort Edward (MP 10), follow Bike "9" until you cross over the railroad and pass Fort Edward High School. Turn right on County Route 37 (Burgoyne). Ride two miles and look for signs identifying the "Glens Falls Feeder Canal Heritage Trail." You'll intersect the trail at a small park. Although you want to turn left, upstream, to Glens Falls, on your immediate right is a remarkable canal site. Here, you'll see a flight of five original locks. These are most interesting and impressive. These five locks were never enlarged and are therefore in their original fifteen-foot width. This is perhaps the best place in New York State where you can get an impression of what a flight of locks of the original "Clinton's Ditch" looked like. I do not recommend following the Feeder Canal eastward, for there is not much to see. Instead, after seeing the combine locks, take the trail westward. It enters Warren County.

The trail follows the towpath (unpaved, but in very good condition) of this historic, virtually "original" segment of canal. Along the way, you'll find excellent interpretive signs explaining the history of this small canal. Don't go so fast that you miss the "Turn Around Basin" at Martindale Street. The Basin was once large enough to hold sixty canalboats. Today it is a small park. Further along, the path switches to the other canal bank.

As the trail enters Glens Falls, there is a short discontinuity. The path ends at Shermantown Road so take Warren Street westward. You'll pass the Hyde Museum. It has an impressive and eclectic collection of art (Botticelli, da Vinci, Rembrandt, Picasso, Whistler, Modigliani, to name but a few!) Further along Warren Street, you'll come to Glen Street. Those who read The Last of the Mohicans, or saw the movie, may recall the cave, beneath a waterfall, where Hawkeye, Cora, Alice, Uncas, Chingachcook, and Major Heyward took refuge. That cave actually exists. It lies beneath the waterfall at

Louis Rossi

Glens Falls Feeder Canal Trail — five combine locks. These locks were never enlarged and represent the look of the original Erie Canal.

Louis Rossi

Glens Falls.To see it, you'll need to go south halfway across the Route 9 bridge.You can see the cave from the walkway. The bridge will take you over the falls that Cooper employed in his narrative; the cave is now beneath the bridge and the site is marked with a marker. Glens Falls is a pleasant small city at the foothills of the Adirondacks. It is a good place for a stop. Be sure to take the two mile "dead end" stretch of the Feeder Canal Trail that extends westward from Glen Street. This is an attractive stretch with additional interpretive signs.

After you visit the Feeder Canal and important attractions of Glens Falls, you must turn north and go through the center of town.You'll want to follow Bay Road until it crosses NY Route 254. Just north of NY Route 254, you'll find the beginning of the rail trail to Lake George, the "Warren County Bikeway." The Warren County Bikeway is being extended south to the Feeder Canal Heritage Trail.

Take the Warren County Bikeway all the way to Lake George. This route is approximately ten miles of excellent paved bikeway. There are two clearly marked and easy to follow on-road segments.

Today's bikepath between Glens Falls and Lake George is built on an old Delaware & Hudson Railway branch line that follows Cooper's "rude path." From Fort Edward to Lake George is approximately fifteen miles, depending on the exact route you follow.

I think that this bikepath is one of the most distinctive, attractive, and historic in all New York. At certain points, it enters dense Adirondack woods that seem as forbidding today as they must have seemed to Cooper's characters. One can easily imagine skillful Indian warriors ambushing redcoats. You'll find that this is quite hilly for a railtrail. As you climb, think of the laboring steam locomotives hauling passenger trains laden with tourists along this route.

You'll enter Lake George Village at Lake George Beach State Park. There are many historic markers in this park; be sure to search them out.This park is filled with "erratics," boulders that clearly don't belong to the terrain in which they are found. It's the glaciers again. These boulders were transported here, in the ice, from regions far to the north. Because the fields around the old fort were never farmed,

Louis Rossi

One of the many historic markers at Lake George.

they lie mostly as the glaciers left them. Lake George once flowed south and into the Hudson River. You are standing on glacial deposits between Lake George Village and Glens Falls which dammed up the lake and reversed its flow so that it now flows north into Lake Champlain and the Saint Lawrence.

Just a short distance ahead is the reconstructed Fort William Henry. This is the end of your tour.

With a base in Lake George, an adventurous cyclist can make a long one-day trip to Ticonderoga via the morning boat, visit the great stone Fort, and cycle back to Lake George via Bike "9" and

Louis Rossi

Boulders (erratics) at the Lake George State Park

Whitehall. This is a tough ride with many major hills. It is a popular ride with local cyclists.

Lake George, too, was once connected to the vast 19th century canal network of New York. But the connection was to Lake Champlain (and the Champlain Canal) at Lake George's northern tip, near Ticonderoga. You can still see some evidence of this old canal in the Village of Ticonderoga.

A Warren and Washington County loop

From Fort Edward, follow the directions immediately above to Lake George. After touring the French and Indian War sites, take NY 9L, northward along the <u>east side</u> (this is very important as you do not want to go up the west shore of the lake). Continue through Cleverdale until you come to NY Route 149. Turn east, toward Fort

Ann. From Fort Ann it will be a ten-mile ride, out-and-back, along Bike "9" to Whitehall, then twelve miles back to Fort Edward. An even more adventurous option would be to use the Lake Shore Steamboat Company's services and take the 38 mile boat ride between Lake George and Baldwin Landing (Ticonderoga), then cycle south from Ticonderoga, through Whitehall, to Fort Edward along Bike "5." Be sure to coordinate your schedule carefully with the boat. Watch out — this one has big hills. In both instances, I recommend making the loop in the "clockwise" direction I have described.

Going North to Canada

From Lake George it is 163 scenic miles to Montreal. If you are continuing north to the Adirondack Park and Canada, I do have one important piece of advice. Take the boat from Lake George Village. While Bike "9" is a pretty flat route, the few short miles north of Whitehall and south of Ticonderoga contain three very steep climbs. It is a very scenic route, great for the climber but difficult for someone loaded with gear. A wise cyclist will trace the invasion routes used by the French and take the magnificent 38-mile boat trip across Lake George. Get the boat in Lake George Village and take it to Baldwin Landing (Fort Ticonderoga). Be sure to make reservations in advance as this boat trip is not daily. It is well worth the time and money. Once off the boat at the north end of Lake George, near the village of Ticonderoga, be sure to visit the Fort (1755). It was the guns from this fort, captured by Ethan Allen, that were hauled overland to George Washington's forces at Boston. Once he had obtained this weaponry, Washington was able to force the British to withdraw from Boston. After the boat ride, the trip to Montreal will be only about 125 miles. From Ticonderoga northward to Montreal, Bike "9" is an excellent rolling route that closely follows Lake Champlain. I've cycled on both shores, both in New York and Vermont. New York is better.

6 / A Post-ride Discussion

Congratulations. In completing this tour, you've accomplished a difficult feat. With 500 miles of canal to see (more if you explore long-abandoned routes), you've overcome a difficult challenge. You should be a bit inspired, too. One has to admire the pioneers who settled the unknown wilderness in hostile times, and had the ambition to build the canals of New York. Whether you've toured the canals on one or two long trips of exploration, or many smaller day trips, you now know a lot about what made New York the "Empire State." We have explored the history of many of the people of upstate New York — both their triumphs such as the Iroquois Confederacy, the Erie Canal and many Revolutionary War victories — and their tragedies, like the story of the Iroquois who remained faithful to the failing British cause, or the lost battles of the War of 1812.

This human story was, as you now know, in large part shaped by geologic forces over 10,000 years ago. Our tours began at a river dramatically shaped by recent glacial erosion into the mighty Hudson River fjord. Both of our tours ended at huge fresh water lakes gouged by those same glaciers. New York's remarkable scenery, climate and agricultural production are very much a result of those geologic forces. It is something unique in North America.

Louis Rossi

Cycling at its best — riding the Canalway Trail.

The last "Ice Age" dramatically affected our recent human history. There is no mountainous barrier between the headwaters of the Saint Lawrence (New France) and the Hudson (Dutch, then British territory). This left us a supremely navigable waterway and no clear natural border. The French and British fortifications that you saw along the ride were built to define that border. They failed miserably; none was a Gibraltar and for over 150 years this region was the site of constant warfare. Here, in the "Cold War" of the 17th and 18th centuries, colonists and their local Indian allies, strengthened by seasoned European troops, fought out the wars of Kings George and Louis. Tens of thousands died in the wilderness here. The cost of these wars bred the Revolution, the loss of American colonies to Great Britain and Canada to France, and the fall of Louis XVI. Indian allies of the French and English were nearly exterminated by the end of these wars. Also among the losers of these wars were both royal families of France and England. Partly by dogged determination, valor and incredible good luck, the winners were the colonists, and we Americans, today.

All of this makes your cycling trips more than just a good day of exercise. I am always amazed at all the interesting things that transpired in the past that change a plain bike ride into a wonderful day cycling. I know that you will revel in this, too, as you cycle by.

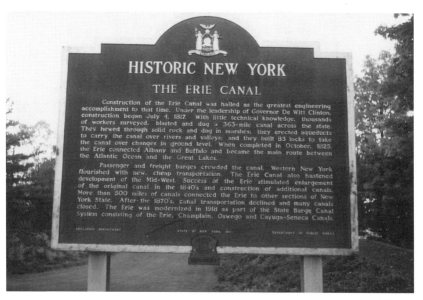

Louis Rossi

One of the many historic markers you saw along the way.

Plan on coming back because still more and more of New York's old canals are being rediscovered and reopened for cyclists to enjoy every year.

R E S O U R C E   G U I D E

APPENDIX I
Map Resources (all are free unless otherwise noted)

"New York State Canalway Trail"   800-4-CANAL-4

"Hudson River Greenway and NYS Bike Route 9"   1-800-CALL-NYS

"Mohawk-Hudson Bikeway: Bike-Hike Trail"   518-447-5660

"Schenectady Cnty Recreation Guide - Mohawk River"   518-386-2225

"Herkimer-Oneida Counties: Bicycle & Pedestrian Routes" 315-798-5037

"Old Erie Canal State Park"   315-687-7821

"Seaway Trail Bicycling" $10.00   800-SEAWAY-T

"Unlock the Legend of Cayuga County's Erie Canal"   315-258-9314

"Unlock the Legend of the Cayuga-Seneca Waterway"   800-4-CANAL

"NY State Canal System: Finger Lakes Region"   800-KIT-4-FUN

"Greater Rochester Area Bike Map,"   716-232-6240

"The Best 100 Miles of the Erie Canal:
Orleans, Monroe and Wayne Counties"   716-546-3070

"Erie Canal Port Guide: Orleans County"   716-589-7004

"Erie Canal: Gateway to the West-Niagara County"   800-338-7890

"Finger Lakes Bike Tours Guide"   GFLRPC   716-442-3786

"Orleans County Trailways and Points of Interest"   716-589-7004

"Bicycle Route Guide: Buffalo/Niagara Falls Area"   716-852-0511

"Warren County Bikeway"   518-623-4141

APPENDIX II
Canal Boat Tour Operators/Navigational Opportunities

There are two important resources:
(1) New York State Passenger Vessel Association,
PO Box 95, Rifton, NY, 12471; 800-852-0095
(2) New York State Canal Corporation, 1-800-4-CANAL-4

There was hardly a famous person in the 19th century who had not taken a boat trip on an Erie Canal packetboat. Charles Dickens said of his trip:

There was much in this mode of traveling which I heartily enjoyed at the time and look back upon with great pleasure...The fast, brisk walk upon the towing path...when every vein and artery seemed to tingle with health; the exquisite beauty of the opening day, when light came glancing off from everything; the gliding on at night so noiselessly.... all these were pure delights. (Quoted from: Stars on the Water, Condon)

Dutch Apple Cruises   518-463-0220
Cruises on the Hudson

Captain JP Cruises   518-270-1901
Various cruises from Troy

Crescent Cruise Line   518-373-1070
Cruises on the Mohawk

The Boat House   518-393-5711
Canoe rentals on the Mohawk

Premier Charters   518-768-2154
Mohawk River and Champlain Canal Tours

Gateway Boat Rides   315-598-BOAT
Canal tours from Sylvan Beach

Mid-Lakes Navigation Co.   800-545-4318

Various canal tours across New York; multi-day tours, and rentals

Mid-Lakes Navigation Company

The "Onondaga" enters Barge Canal Lock 24 at Baldwinsville.

Liberty Boat Tours   315-946-4108

Tours from Lyons

Colonial Belle   716-377-4600

Canal tours from Fairport

Fairport Lady   716-223-1930

Canal tours from Fairport

Amherst Marine Center   716-691-6707

Boat rentals

Corn Hill Navigation   716-262-5661

Tours near Rochester

Waterway USA   716-352-8687
Tours near Spencerport

Apple Grove Inn   716-798-2323
Mule-drawn packet boats from Medina

Lockport Locks & Erie Canal Cruises 800-378-0352
Tours through Lockport locks

Maid of the Mist Boat Tours   716-284-8897
Tours of Niagara Falls

Miss Buffalo/Niagara Clipper   716-856-6696
Tours from Buffalo and Tonawanda

American Canadian Caribbean Line 800-556-7450
Tours of the entire canal system

Lake George Steamboat Company   800-553-BOAT
Various tours; one way trip across Lake George

Champlain Canal Tour Boats   518-695-5496
Tours from Schuylerville

Lake Champlain Ferries   802-864-9804
Three ferry routes across Lake Champlain

Fort Ticonderoga Ferry   802-897-7999
Ferry at Ft. Ticonderoga

APPENDIX III
Historical Sites – Important Contacts

Hudson Mohawk Industrial Gateway	518-274-5267
New York State Canal Corporation	800-4-CANAL-4
New York State Dept. of Transportation	888-BIKE-NYS
New York State Division of Tourism	800-CALL-NYS
NYS Office of Parks and Recreation	518-474-0456
NYS Department of Ag and Markets	518-457-4188
New York State Passenger Vessel Association	800-852-0095
Albany Urban Cultural Park Visitors Center	518-434-5132
Albany Convention and Visitors Bureau	518-434-1217
Schuyler Mansion	518-434-0834
Ten Broeck Mansion	518-436-9826
Historic Cherry Hill	518-434-4791
New York State Museum	518-474-5877
Riverspark/Cohoes Visitors Center	518-237-7999
Rensselaer County Tourism	518-270-2900
Schenectady Urban Cultural Park	518-382-5417
Schenectady Cnty Chamber of Commerce	518-372-5656
Glen Sanders Mansion	518-374-7762
Montgomery Cnty. Chamber of Commerce	518-842-8200
Guy Park State Historic Site	518-842-7550
Shrine of the North American Martyrs	518-853-3033
Johnson Hall State Historic Site	518-762-8712
Canajoharie Library and Art Gallery	518-673-2314
Schoharie Crossing State Historic Site	518-829-7516
Fort Plain Museum	518-993-2527
Fort Klock Historic Restoration	518-568-7779
Herkimer Cnty Tourist Information Center	315-369-6983
Herkimer Home State Historic Site	315-823-0398
Oriskany Battlefield State Historic Site	315-768-7224

NYS Office of Parks and Recreation/Capitol Region

An encampment at Johnson Hall State Historic Site.

Remington Firearms Museum	800-243-9700
Oneida County Visitors Bureau	800-426-3132
Fort Stanwix National Monument	315-336-2090
Erie Canal Village	315-337-3999
Madison County Tourism	315-684-7320
Erie Canal State Park	315-637-6111
Canastota Canal Town Museum	315-697-3451
Chittenango Landing Canal Boat Museum	315-687-3801
Syracuse Convention and Visitors Bureau	315-470-1910
Erie Canal Museum	315-471-0593
Oswego County Department of Tourism	315-349-8322
Fort Ontario State Historic Site	315-343-4711
The Seaway Trail	800-Seaway-T
Cayuga County Tourism	315-258-9314
Montezuma National Wildlife Refuge	315-568-5987
National Women's Hall of Fame	315-568-8060

Woman's Rights National Historical Park   315-568-2991
Wayne County Public Information Office   315-946-5470
Hill Cumorah Visitors Center   315-597-5851
Ganondagan State Historic Site   716-924-5848
Greater Rochester Visitors Bureau   716-546-3070
Genesee Valley Greenway   www.netacc.net/~fogvg
Canalside Inn   716-352-6784
Cobblestone Museum, Albion   716-589-9013
Holley Depot Museum, Holley   716-638-6333
Medina Railroad Exhibit Center, Medina   716-798-6106
Orleans County Tourism   716-589-3199
Niagara County Tourism   716-439-7300
Schoellkopf Geological Museum   716-278-1780
Old Fort Niagara   716-745-7611
Greater Buffalo Visitors Bureau   716-852-0511
Bicycle Museum   716-662-3853

Saratoga County Chamber of Commerce   518-584-3255
Saratoga National Historical Park
(Battlefield and Gen. Schuyler House)   518-664-9821
Warren County Tourism Department   518-761-6366
Washington County Tourism   518-746-2290
Old Fort House Museum at Fort Edward   518-747-9600
Fort William Henry   518-668-5471
Fort Ticonderoga   518-585-2821
Lake Champlain Bikeways   518-597-4212
Lake Champlain Visitors Center   518-597-4646

Other Books from Vitesse Press

Cycling Health and Physiology by Ed Burke, PH.D. $17.95
Using sports science to improve your riding and racing

Bicycle Road Racing by Edward Borysewicz $24.95
A complete road-racing program by former National Coach Eddie B.

Road Racing: Technique & Training by Bernard Hinault $17.95
Racing and training tips from a five-time Tour de France winner.

Massage For Cyclists by Roger Pozeznik $14.95
Clear advice and excellent photos of massage sequences. 2nd Printing.

Mountain Biking For Women by Robin Stuart & Cathy Jensen $15.00
Woman to woman advice and instruction from two experienced cyclists.

Central New York Mountain Biking by Dick Mansfield $12.95
Thirty of the best back road and trail rides in upstate New York.

Vermont Mountain Biking by Dick Mansfield $10.95
Twenty-four rides in southern Vermont.

Fit and Pregnant by Joan Butler $16.00
Advice from a nurse-midwife who is an athlete and mother.

Runner's Guide To Cross Country Skiing by Dick Mansfield $10.95
Still the best source for runners looking for a winter alternative.

Canoe Racing by Peter Heed $14.95
The "bible" of flat water canoe racing. Third printing.

We encourage you to buy our books at a bookstore or sports shop. When ordering directly from Vitesse, prepayment or a credit card number and expiration date is required. Please include the price of the book plus handling ($2.50 for the first book, $1.00 for each additional book) and 5% sales tax for Maryland addresses.

Telephone   301-772-5915   Fax   301-772-5921

Postal Orders: VITESSE PRESS, 4431 Lehigh Road, #288,
College Park, MD 20740
Email: dickmfield@aol.com   Web site: www.acornpub.com